D0731326

MAKING WOODEN
# TOYS & GAMES

*Rayleen Beger*

# MAKING WOODEN
# TOYS & GAMES

## Jeff and Jennie Loader

Guild of Master Craftsman Publications Ltd

First published 1995 by
Guild of Master Craftsman Publications Ltd
166 High Street, Lewes
East Sussex BN7 1XU

© Jeff and Jennie Loader 1995

ISBN 0 946819 55 6

Photographs on front cover, back cover (top) and page 21 by Zul Mukhida
All other photographs by Jennie Loader
Illustrations by Jeff Loader

All rights reserved.

The right of Jeff and Jennie Loader to be identified as the authors of this work has been asserted in accordance with the Copyright Designs and Patents Act 1988, Sections 77 and 78.

No part of this publication may be reproduced, stored in a retrieval system, or transmitted in any form or by any means without the prior permission of the publisher and copyright owner.

This book is sold subject to the condition that all designs are copyright and are not for commercial reproduction without permission of the designer and copyright owner.

The publishers and authors can accept no legal responsibility for any consequences arising from the application of information, advice or instructions given in this publication. None of the finished toys or games are suitable for children under 36 months.

Designed by Gellatly Norman Associates

Typeset by Central Southern Typesetters, Eastbourne

Printed and bound in Singapore under the supervision of MRM Graphics, Winslow, Buckinghamshire, UK

## DEDICATION

*To the child in all of us*

## ACKNOWLEDGEMENTS

*Our grateful thanks go out to the following: all our family and friends for their views, ideas, toy testing sessions and general support.*

*The following companies, who have generously supported our venture: Avon Plywood Limited; Britain's Petite Limited; Hobbies (Dereham) Limited; J D Woodward; W Hobby Limited; C & H Fabrics (Brighton) and Cade Craft (Lewes).*

*Liz Inman and all at GMC Publications Limited for their belief in our abilities and support throughout the writing of this book.*

*A special thank you must go to Luke, our son, who has been our chief toy tester and critic!*

# Contents

| | | |
|---|---|---|
| Introduction | 1 |
| 1 | Materials | 2 |
| 2 | Tools | 4 |
| 3 | Construction Techniques | 10 |
| 4 | Painting & Finishing | 18 |
| 5 | Arthur's Tower | 23 |
| 6 | Broomstick Racers | 39 |

| | | |
|---|---|---|
| 7 | Butterfly Mobile | 43 |
| 8 | Wall-mounted Chessboard | 47 |
| 9 | Chris Clown's Crazy Car | 53 |
| 10 | Flying Kite | 63 |
| 11 | Freda the Frog | 67 |
| 12 | Gymnast | 71 |
| 13 | Hang-on-Hank & Bucking Billy | 77 |

| 14 | Classic Racing | 83 | 21 | Yo-Yos | 141 |
| 15 | Horseshoe Hurling | 97 | 22 | Theatre | 145 |
| 16 | Loader's Garage | 103 | 23 | 18-Wheeler Lorry & Tractors | 155 |
| 17 | Marvellous Mighty Mervyn | 111 | | Glossary | 165 |
| 18 | Monster Pick-ups | 119 | | Metric Conversion Table | 166 |
| 19 | Shove Ha'penny | 127 | | About the Authors | 167 |
| 20 | Skittle Alley Skittlers | 133 | | | |

**Please note:** *within the instructions given in this book, the pronoun 'he' has been used. This is purely for convenience and consistency; it is not our intention to exclude or offend lady readers.*

# Introduction

Throughout the ages wooden toys have been made, often by hand, at home, for the children of the family. With the aid of this book, you will be able to continue this age-old tradition. It is our belief that however many computerized space-age toys and games come onto the market, wooden toys will always have a strong appeal.

The range of projects chosen for inclusion in this book is wide, the intention being to bridge the gap between the simple appeal of a traditional wooden toy and the excitement of the latest megatyre-squealing laser-zapping toy! You may recognize a few of the toys and games as old favourites; others have been specially devised and designed for this book. Some have been specifically designed with economy of space and storage in mind while ensuring that their play value is not reduced.

Those adults among us who still delight in playing have not been forgotten. Several of the toys and games included will appeal to the more mature reader – our friends and ourselves certainly enjoy playing with some of the projects when the kids are safely tucked up in bed!

When planning the contents of this book we have tried to ensure that all keen toy makers have been catered for, whether novices or old hands. Some of the projects are quick and straightforward, and can be successfully completed using a minimum of materials and tools. Some are suitable for children to make, given adequate adult supervision. Other projects present more of a challenge and require time, patience and practised skills to complete.

Whichever projects you choose to undertake, we hope you will enjoy making them, and playing with the end result!

ONE
# Materials

In this chapter, and in the following two chapters on tools and construction techniques, we have provided guidelines for the construction of all the projects contained within this book. There is a descriptive list of the main materials and tools required. Some of the construction processes, such as fretsawing, rivet jointing etc., are described in depth. However, these sections do not, and cannot fairly be expected to, instruct the reader in every process and workshop practice.

If you are at all unsure of how to use a tool, or undertake a task correctly, please seek some expert advice. Many colleges run evening classes that can instruct you. There are also many excellent books available to inform you.

## Plywood

The main bulk of the toys and games contained within this book are constructed from plywood.

We find that birch plywood is an ideal material to use: it is strong, stable and has fine straight-grained surface faces. Various thicknesses are available, the following being used in this book: 1.5mm ($1/16$in), 3mm ($1/8$in), 6mm ($1/4$in), 9mm ($3/8$in) and 12mm ($1/2$in).

The latter two thicknesses are usually sold in 2,440 × 1,220mm (8 × 4ft) sheets. The smaller thicknesses are also available in large sheets, but more manageable sizes, e.g. 600 × 300mm (24 × 12in) can be obtained from hobbyist suppliers.

If you are new to toy making, or you are unsure how much toy making you intend to do, it is advisable to buy the smaller sheets first.

Smaller thicknesses can be glued together to produce larger ones: 3mm ($1/8$in) + 6mm ($1/4$in) = 9mm ($3/8$in). This technique should only be used for the construction of small components – fortunately, in toy making, most are!

## Hardboard

A relatively small amount of standard hardboard is required. It is used as a less expensive alternative to birch plywood for the roofs of Loader's Garage.

Hardboard is readily available from timber merchants and most DIY suppliers.

## Wooden moulding

Wooden mouldings, in a variety of styles, can be purchased from most timber merchants and DIY suppliers. They are frequently available in either softwoods or hardwoods.

## Hardwood

Some of the projects require certain components to be produced from a suitable hardwood. Beech is ideal for this purpose. Many good timber merchants have a section of small strips and offcuts. As the components required are relatively small in size, there is no need to buy large quantities of hardwood.

## Dowel rods

Round-sectioned lengths of softwood and hardwood dowel rods are available in a variety of diameters from timber merchants, DIY stores and hobbyist outlets.

It is advisable to use hardwood doweling for the smaller diameters required as this is stronger than softwood.

## Abrasive paper

You will find it necessary to keep a stock of an assortment of grades, from very fine to coarse, of abrasive paper.

Aluminium oxide paper and silicon carbide paper (known as wet-and-dry paper) are the ideal types to use.

## Sanding sticks

These are a useful aid when sanding intricate shapes or surfaces which are not easily accessible. They are simply constructed from thin strips of birch plywood, with abrasive paper glued onto them.

You can amass a useful range of different lengths, widths and abrasive grades. The most useful thicknesses of plywood for this purpose are 3mm (⅛in) and 6mm (¼in). If you use anything thinner than this, such as 1.5mm (¹⁄₁₆in), be extremely careful as these may bend or snap when in use.

## Wire wool

Wire wool is a useful item to keep at hand, 0000 grade being particularly useful for lightly sanding (or de-nibbing) a varnished or painted finish prior to applying the final coat.

## Glue

PVA adhesive (or 'white glue') is used for any gluing necessary in the construction of the toys and games. It usually comes in conveniently sized bottles with a nozzle top.

## Pins

A variety of small moulding, panel and/or fret pins are required.

## Miscellaneous

A variety of other items will be required, for example, wooden wheels, buttons, hinges, steel axles, wood balls, beads etc. Most are available from hobbyist suppliers.

## Filler

After moulding pins have been driven below the surface of the wood using a pin punch, you will need to fill the resulting recess with filler.

There are many brands, types and shades of wood filler on the market. Choose one that suits your particular needs best. If in doubt, most retail outlets will advise you.

# Tools

## Pencils

We have granted pencils premier position in this section, as they are one of the most important and oft neglected of hand tools!

Compared with the cost of other tools pencils are inexpensive, so try to use good quality ones. We find 2H pencils to be an ideal compromise between a softer grade (which gives a nice bold line, but blunts much too easily) and a harder grade (which does not blunt so easily, but may indent the wood too readily and does not draw a bold line so well).

Accurate measuring and marking out is absolutely essential, so it is vital that you always keep a sharp point on your pencil. It is amazing how many people fail to do this!

**Tip**  To sharpen a pencil well, using a sharp knife, first pare the wood away from around the lead at an acute angle until a reasonable length of lead is exposed. Then, sharpen the lead to a regular point either with a small file or fine abrasive paper. If using abrasive paper, lay it on a flat surface and rub the lead frequently across it.

## Rules

You will need a 300mm (12in) and, if possible, a 600mm (24in) steel rule.

## Retractable measuring tape

A retractable measuring tape, preferably one with a locking device, is useful when measuring large lengths and widths. A 3m (10ft) size is a useful length to own.

## Try squares

For marking and checking 90° angles.

A traditional woodworkers' try square has a steel blade with a hardwood stock incorporating a brass edge.

A combination square is more versatile, as it measures and tests mitres as well as levels and squareness. The blade is usually adjustable in length.

A small steel engineers' precision square, 50mm (2in) or 100mm (4in) in size, is more manageable when checking the squareness of small work.

## Knives

You will find a craft/modellers' knife or a scalpel invaluable for various cutting and trimming tasks.

*Fig 2.1*
**Nine-inch try square with wood and brass stock (top), 2-inch engineers' try square (centre), combination square (right), and 6-inch try square with wood and brass stock (left).**

Fig 2.2
**Block plane (left) and smoothing plane (right).**

## Planes

A smoothing plane is useful to have, but not essential. As the majority of planing operations involve relatively small pieces of plywood, we recommend a block plane is used.

A block plane has its blade set at a lower angle, thus allowing it to trim plywood edges (which include end-grain faces) cleanly and easily.

If you do not already own one, we recommend that you buy one. Although they may seem expensive, it is well worth purchasing a top-of-the-range model that has a depth-adjustment screw and a throat-adjustment lever. The cheaper, and less sophisticated, models are not so simple to adjust and may prove tiresome to use.

## Chisels

Only a couple of chisels are required to construct the projects in this book. 6mm (¼in) and 10mm (⅜in) and/or 12mm (½in). Either firmer or bevel-edge are acceptable.

## Handsaws

Apart from a fretsaw (see pages 11–13) you will require a fine-toothed crosscut saw and a fine-toothed back saw.

Crosscut saw
It is preferable to use a panel saw, which is a large handsaw that has fine teeth, usually 10–12 points per inch (PPI). This makes it an ideal tool for cutting out larger sheets of plywood.

Fig 2.3
**Crosscut saw (top), tenon saw (centre) and dovetail saw (bottom).**

### Back saw

Out of the range of back saws the tenon saw is probably the most versatile, with 13–15 PPI. However, if possible, a finer-toothed back saw, such as a dovetail saw (22 PPI+) is desirable, especially when cutting small toy components.

### Hacksaw

A junior hacksaw is needed for cutting the steel axle rods and rivets.

## Hammers

The majority of hammering tasks required involve the driving of moulding pins. Therefore, a lightweight pin hammer should suffice.

If you intend to construct any of the projects requiring riveting, a light- to middle-weight ball-peen hammer will be required.

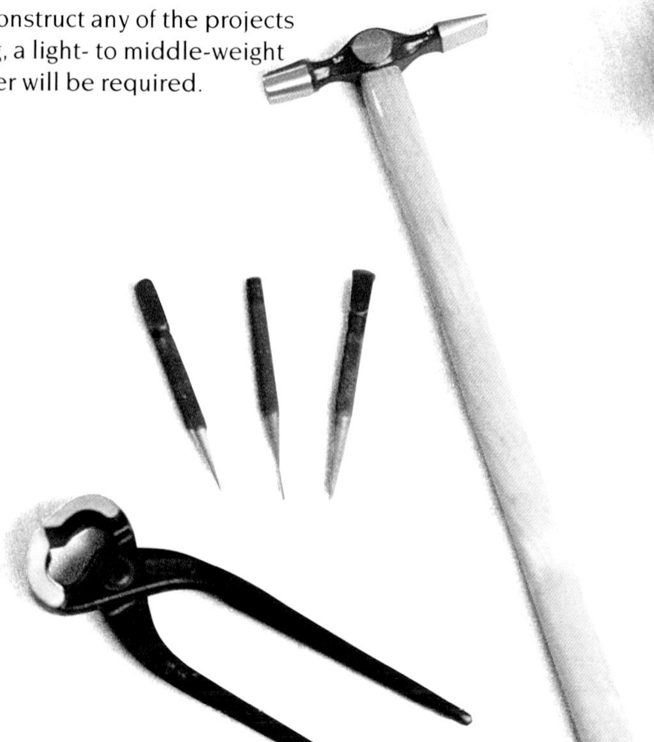

## Pincers

Pincers will be required for removing any pins that bend during driving.

## Screwdrivers

A couple of the smaller sized straight-tip variety will be required to fit the variety of small brass screws used (see **page 8**).

*Fig 2.5*
**Marking gauge.**

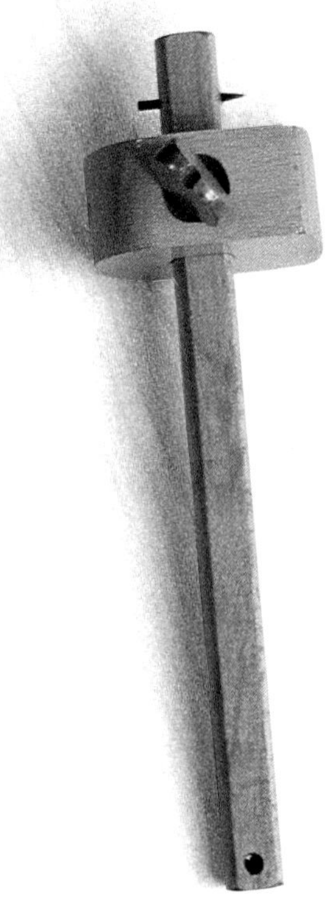

*Fig 2.4*
**From top to bottom: pin hammer, nail sets and pin punches, and pincers.**

## Pin punch

This is used for driving pins slightly below the surface of the timber prior to filling. Use a punch marginally smaller in diameter than the pin head.

## Marking gauge

An invaluable tool when a line needs to be marked parallel to a square edge.

## Hand drill

For many, the portable power drill has replaced the need for this tool. However, the hand drill has many advantages over a power drill. For example, the hand drill is usually lighter in weight and therefore easier to handle. It is also easier to control when drilling small holes (such as pilot holes for small

screws) on intricate items, as you can stop the bit cutting instantly as you desire to do so. A hand-held portable power drill inevitably runs on for a short while after the power has been shut off.

The hand drill is ideal for many toy making operations, and we thoroughly recommend purchasing one.

## Drill bits

You will need a variety of these. It is a good idea to have a range of bits the size of which are in between and around the diameters most frequently used in toy making. These are: 1.5mm ($^1/_{16}$in), 3mm ($^1/_8$in), 6mm ($^1/_4$in) and 10mm ($^3/_8$in).

For example, when drilling a hole to receive 3mm ($^1/_8$in) dowel, you may find that the diameter of the actual dowel is considerably oversized. As reducing this diameter can prove problematical, a simple solution is to drill the hole fractionally larger, say 3.3mm. If all else fails, the diameter of the dowel *can* be reduced by judicious sanding. Be careful, however, to sand equally round the dowel in the area you want to reduce, or you may end up with a wobbly fit.

*Fig 2.6*
**Hand drill (right), drill twist bits (centre) and drill zip bits (left).**

There are two main types of bit: conventional twist bits and dowel bits.

Dowel bits, as the name suggests, are specially designed to drill a flat-bottomed hole to receive dowels. They are similar to a twist bit except that they have a central lead point and two cutting spurs. This enables the bits to cut through wood without being deflected by the grain.

## Zip bits

These are also known as spade bits or flat bits. They must be used in conjunction with a power drill.

Each bit has a long central lead point that enables it to be fed positively through the workpiece. They are usually available in sizes ranging from 6mm ($^1/_4$in) to 38mm (1$^1/_2$in).

## Awl

An awl is useful for marking the centre point of holes prior to drilling, and for boring a starting hole for small screws.

## Bench hook

This is a useful workbench aid used when sawing timber with a back saw.

They are usually made from scrap wood rather than being shop bought (see **Fig 2.8**).

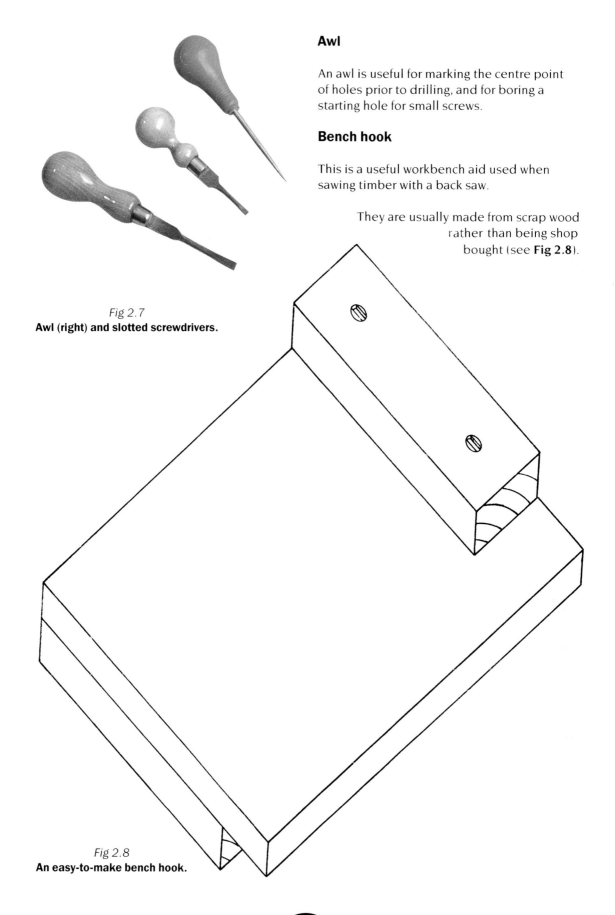

*Fig 2.7*
**Awl (right) and slotted screwdrivers.**

*Fig 2.8*
**An easy-to-make bench hook.**

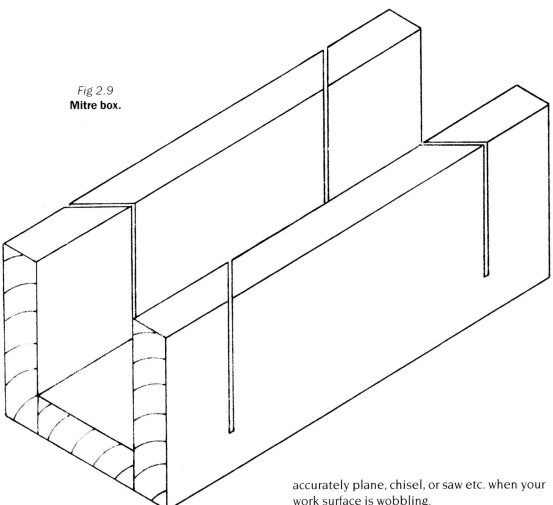

*Fig 2.9*
**Mitre box.**

## Mitre box

Used for cutting mitres on the edging. There are numerous jigs and aids available to enable accurate mitres to be cut, and a mitre box is one of the most inexpensive. They are usually made from hardwood, e.g. beech (see **Fig 2.9**).

## Workbench

Workbenches come in various shapes and sizes. Although there are many varieties available on the market, many craftsmen use home-built ones.

Whether built-in or free-standing, your workbench should be stable. It is difficult to

accurately plane, chisel, or saw etc. when your work surface is wobbling.

Equally, the vice you use should be firmly secured to the workbench. Do not worry if you do not possess a large, top-of-the-range, quick-release one. A simple, good quality medium-sized vice is adequate for toy making.

## G-cramps

These are useful for holding workpieces together while waiting for glue to dry.

## Portable power tools and machinery

Except for a powered fretsaw and, for some of the projects, a drill and stand (or pillar drill) you should not need any other power tools or machinery.

Of course, if you possess and are conversant with the safe use of other power tools, do feel free to use them where appropriate.

THREE
# Construction Techniques

## Dividing a line

For some of the projects you will need to divide a line or workpiece into equal parts. Here is an example of a quick and easy method to use without having to use figure measurements (see **Fig 3.1**).

**1** Suppose you want to divide a line, AB, into equal parts. Draw a line (AC) away from one end of the line to be divided. This may be at any suitable angle (see **Fig 3.1(a)**).

**2** Set dividers or a compass to any reasonable size that will not make the number of divisions required exceed the length of the newly drawn line when marked.

**3** Mark the line with the dividers or compass to the number of divisions required. In the example shown it is four, labelled D, E, F and G.

**4** Place a set square against the edge of a rule. The rule must be parallel to the line being divided. Join up the last mark (G) with the end of the line (B). Move the set square along the rule and draw parallel lines from the marks D, E, F and G (see **Fig 3.1(b)**). The original line should now be equally divided into the number of parts required.

This method is particularly useful if you are making Arthur's Tower, which requires equal divisions in order to make the castellations.

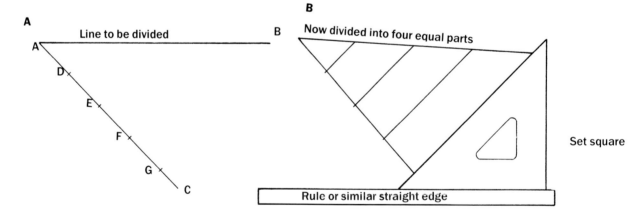

Fig 3.1
**Dividing a line into equal parts.**

## Fretsawing

Fretsawing is utilized many times during the construction of the toys in this book. We have gone into some detail for those new to fretsawing and have included tips and techniques.

Fretsawing can be an enjoyable practice and often becomes a popular pastime in its own right.

Basically, fretsawing is the process of cutting small curves and shapes from wood with a thin, narrow blade. There are two main categories of fretsawing: hand powered and machine powered.

### Hand fretsawing

A hand-held fretsaw has a deep bowed metal frame. The spring of the frame holds the blade under tension. The blade is clamped to the frame by two thumbscrews. The blade is usually fitted with its teeth pointing towards the handle, as it cuts on the downstroke.

It is best to sit at the workbench when cutting. The work should be supported by a jig which is clamped to the edge of the bench. Ready-made jigs may be purchased, or jigs can easily be made from some scrap plywood (see **Figs 3.2–3.3**). Make the dimensions of the jig to your own requirements.

Alternatively, a more substantial jig can be made, also from scrap plywood. This is held in the workbench vice while in use (see **Fig 3.4**). Again, the size of the jig will depend upon your requirements. The longer back-piece of the jig will enable height adjustment and give clearance between your hand and the vice top on each downstroke cut.

With a little practice, cutting with a hand-held fretsaw should not prove too difficult. Never force the blade through the work, and try to maintain a smooth, rhythmical cutting action.

When cutting internal shapes and holes, drill a hole through the waste part first. Then unclamp one end of the blade, pass it through the hole, reclamp the blade and begin cutting.

*Fig 3.2*
**Two very simple fretsawing platforms that can be made of scrap plywood.**

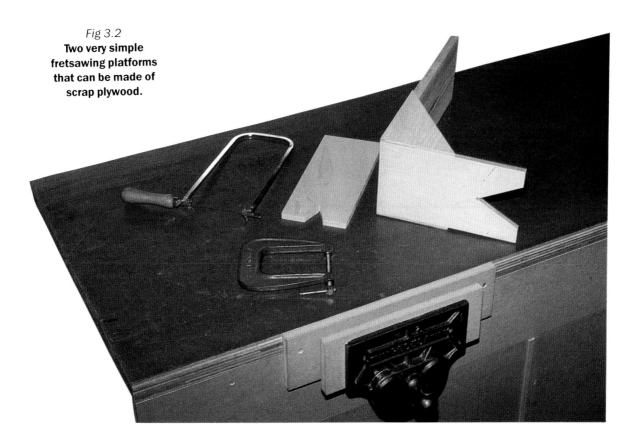

Fig 3.3
**This home-made jig is simply clamped to the workbench.**

## Machine fretsawing

If you intend to make wooden toys regularly and were given the option of owning only one machine, then a fretsaw machine would prove a wise choice.

It is one of the most versatile machines in the workshop. Many models can cut intricate curves in various materials such as plywood, hardwoods and softwoods, plastics and some metals. Some machines have the capability of tilting their cutting table to 45°. Often the blades may be turned through 90°, enabling long cuts to be made. Some manufacturers supply machines with variable speed control, which is a very useful feature.

Fig 3.4
**A slightly more elaborate jig; its height can be adjusted.**

Most fretsaws are powered by a small and (usually) relatively quiet electric motor, but there are one or two treadle machines on the market. These are comparatively inexpensive machines with the added plus that they help you keep fit as you have to pedal them with your feet to drive the blade! Don't scoff if you have not come across one of these machines before – they require little maintenance, are economical, quiet and produce a fine finish of cut.

Generally, when using a powered fretsaw, let the blade cut freely and do not force the workpiece into it. Choose the correct type of blade for the job in hand (see '**Fretsaw blades', below**). Always try to keep your hands to either side of the blade, never put them directly in front of the cutting edge. If necessary, especially on thin work, use a hold-down clamp to help stop the workpiece from vibrating while cutting.

Wear an appropriate dust mask during cutting operations.

When cutting tight curves or corners, it is easy to imagine that the blade will run away and cut off course before you can turn the workpiece. Remember that this should not happen if you are feeding the workpiece into the machine at the correct speed. You should be able to stop the workpiece when you get to a tight corner and the blade should idle quite happily without cutting. You may then ease the workpiece around so the blade turns the corner and off you go again.

A good fretsaw machine should produce an even and smooth cut, leaving the workpiece requiring little or no sanding in order to smooth the edges.

All the projects requiring fretsawing have been made using the Diamond Heavy Duty Fretsaw. This has proved to be a strongly constructed, versatile machine capable of a variety of cutting applications.

### Fretsaw blades

There are various types of blades, but for the projects contained within this book we need only concern ourselves with skip-tooth (widely spaced teeth) blades. These come in different grades, usually 00–11 teeth per inch (TPI). Always buy good quality blades and try to keep plenty in stock.

The table below will help you choose the correct blade to use.

| Fretsaw Blade Sizes/Usage | | |
|---|---|---|
| **Grade** | **TPI** | **Material and Thickness Capability** |
| 00 | 27 | veneers and wood up to 3mm (⅛in) |
| 0 | 26 | same as above |
| 1 | 25 | 3mm (⅛in) wood |
| 2 | 20 | 4.5mm (³⁄₁₆in) wood |
| 3 | 19 | 6mm (¼in) wood |
| 4 | 18 | 10mm (⅜in) wood |
| 5 | 17 | 12mm (½in) wood |
| 6 | 16 | 18mm (¾in) wood |
| 7 | 15 | |
| 9 | 13 | larger thicknesses – |
| 10 | 12 | from 18mm (¾in) to |
| 11 | 10 | 50mm (2in) wood |

## Riveting

Some of the toys, such as Hang-on-Hank, Freda Frog etc, have jointed limbs. An unusual method of loose riveting has been used to enable the free movement of these limbs.

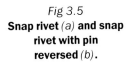

*Fig 3.5*
**Snap rivet** (a) **and snap rivet with pin reversed** (b)**.**

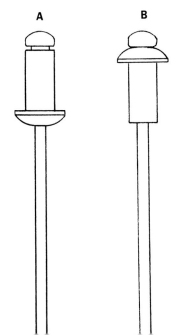

The rivets used are called snap rivets (see **Fig 3.5**) and are available in a variety of lengths and widths. It is advisable to obtain a few of varying sizes, as you will find that bigger rivets are more suited to bigger jointing tasks than smaller ones and vice versa.

Normally snap rivets are fixed with a hand-operated riveter. For the construction of the toys in this book the use of one of these will not be necessary.

As an example of the technique required, the jointing of Hang-on-Hank's arms is described below. Please note that this process of riveting may sound difficult and tedious to those who have not done it before. However, it really is a surprisingly quick and neat method of loose jointing some of the toys!

### Loose-riveting method

**Items required:**
An assortment of snap rivets
A small ball-peen hammer
A small hacksaw
A metal-working vice
A home-made rivet set (optional)

Take two 4.0mm × 5.6mm snap rivets (see **Fig 3.5(a)**). Using a hammer, tap out the central pin of each rivet. Hold the rivets in a vice when doing this. Now slide one of the rivet pins back into position, but make sure that it is reversed as in Fig 3.5(b).

Make sure that all the holes drilled into Hank's body parts are of a suitable size to enable free movement when riveted. Drill trial holes of different sizes in scrap wood to determine the perfect drill diameter to suit your chosen rivets.

Pass the newly assembled rivet through the appropriate arm and Hank's body.

Take the disassembled rivet head, pass it through the other arm and thread this onto the other rivet's pin. This pin should be protruding out of the arm hole in Hank's body. You should now have the arrangement shown in Fig 3.6.

Make the protruding pin a little way away from

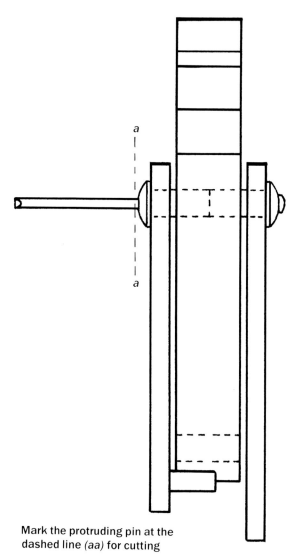

Mark the protruding pin at the dashed line *(aa)* for cutting

*Fig 3.6*
**Front view of Hank's
body and arms showing
rivet assembly.**

the domed rivet head. This is the point where you will cut the pin (see **Fig 3.6**). The remaining short length of pin is to be riveted over. Experience will tell you where to cut the pin. Practise riveting some scrap wood first if unsure.

With the pin marked, disassemble the arms and body, hold the pin in the vice and cut to length. Then reassemble the arms, body and rivet arrangement.

The small protruding length of pin must now be hammered over to hold the entire assembly together. To do this, the pin's round head should be placed on a hard metal surface. Alternatively, a home-made set can be made by drilling a very shallow hole (to form a cup-like depression) into the top surface of the head of a large bolt. The hole should just allow the round rivet pin head to fit snugly into it.

Securely hold the set in a vice and place Hank onto it.

Using the ball end of the hammer, repeatedly gently tap the protruding pin. You must try to round the pin over on all sides and fill the slight countersunk hole that most rivet heads have. When complete, check that you haven't left any sharp edges on the pin.

Hank's arms should now move freely. If they are too stiff, or they will not move at all, this can easily be rectified by drilling the rivets out and re-riveting.

To do this, centre-punch the newly hammered end. Then use a suitably sized drill bit and drill this out, thus enabling the assembly to come apart.

On some riveting tasks you may find that the shanks of your rivets are too long and protrude too much from your workpiece. This would create much too loose a fit. Therefore, simply cut or file away any surplus before fitting.

## Drilling

The process of drilling accurate holes is required for most of the toys. Provided you use the appropriate bits (see 'Drill Bits', page 7), drilling should be a relatively straightforward process.

Whether you own a large pillar drill or a vertical drill stand and power drill, or if you have a hand drill or brace, a few simple precautions should be taken.

Always ensure that the workpiece is firmly held, preferably in a vice or by a cramp, while drilling takes place.

Beware of loose clothing, jewellery, hair or

electric cables coming near the drilling operation.

Always wear eye protection (and ear protection, if necessary). Also, wear a dust mask appropriate to the material being drilled.

Make sure that you drilling equipment is in good order and that your drill/boring bits are sharp.

When using any type of drill press, ensure that it is bolted securely to a stable, solid surface.

When you are drilling right through a piece of wood, place a scrap piece at the back or base of it. This will help prevent splintering when the bit breaks through the workpiece.

When a hole needs to be drilled partway through the workpiece to a precise depth, some means of gauging the depth is required. Large drill presses and vertical drill stands often have a depth gauge and a depth stop fitted. The latter, when set, will prevent the drill from going deeper when the correct depth has been obtained.

If your drill does not have this feature, or you are using a hand drill, you can indicate the desired depth by wrapping a piece of coloured sticky tape around the drill bit. The depth required will be the distance from the tip of the drill bit spurs (if using a wood bit) to the leading edge of the sticky tape. Stop drilling when the leading edge of the sticky tape reaches the surface of the workpiece (see **Fig 3.7**).

## Fitting wheels

Two types of wheels are used for the projects in this book: wooden and plastic wheels.

### Wooden wheels

The wooden wheels are pre-made and are fixed using hardwood doweling for axles. You may, of course, make your own wooden wheels, but the pre-made ones are inexpensive, readily available and save you a lot of time.

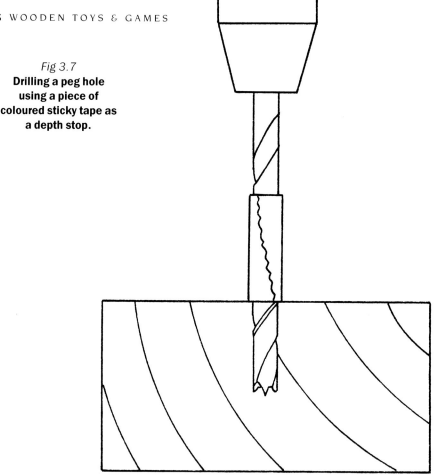

*Fig 3.7*
**Drilling a peg hole using a piece of coloured sticky tape as a depth stop.**

To fit wooden wheels to, for example, a four-wheeled toy, you will first need to make two axle rods. For the majority of the projects these are cut from 6mm (¼in) hardwood doweling. Choose a suitable length of dowel and sand it smooth.

You will notice that the relevant projects do not give the exact length of axle required. This is for the simple reason that, because of slightly varying thicknesses of wheels, plywood, washers etc., your components may differ slightly from the ones we used when making up the projects. To find out the length of wooden axle required, follow these steps:

**1** Square off the sanded length of dowel.
**2** Drill out the centres of the wheels to a diameter size that allows the axle to fit positively and firmly. Ensure that each wheel is held securely by a vice or cramping device during drilling.
**3** Thread a wheel onto the axle so the squared end is flush with the outside of the wheel.

**4** If a washer is to be fitted (this ensures that the wheel will turn freely and not rub against the side of the vehicle), thread this onto the axle.
**5** Pass this axle assembly through the axle hole of the toy. This axle hole should be drilled to a diameter size that allows the axle to turn easily and freely.
**6** Fit a washer and a wheel onto the axle at the other side of the toy.
**7** Allow a small gap (about 1mm) between the wheel and the washer, and the washer and the toy. These gaps will ensure that the wheels will turn freely.
**8** With a pencil, mark the axle at the point it needs to be cut to be flush with the outside of the wheel.
**9** Disassemble the axle.
**10** Cut the axle rod squarely to length.
**11** Reassemble, this time gluing the wheels into position.

**Note** It is advisable to paint all the necessary components prior to final assembly.

## Plastic wheels

Plastic wheels are fitted in a similar manner to wooden wheels, except that steel axle rods are used and spring hubcaps are fixed to the ends of the axles to retain the wheels.

Use a junior hacksaw to cut the axle rod. File away any sharp edges.

Remember to allow enough length for the spring hubcaps to be attached.

If you have never fitted these type of hubcaps before, practise on a surplus length of axle rod first. A few light taps with a hammer is all that is required to fit the cap to the rod. Do not try to fit them with one large blow from the hammer as you will probably find that the hub cap will 'ping' off across the workshop and your hammer will slip, damaging the workpiece.

In some instances, both wood and plastic wheels may be fitted using round-head screws. This practice is not ideal; the axle method is much stronger and more stable.

## Dowel joints

In some of the projects it is suggested that a glue joint be reinforced using dowel pegs. You may be familiar with this jointing method from furniture making, where it is primarily used for carcass joints, framing joints and edge-to-edge joints.

The diameter of the pegs required for these joints depends upon the thickness of timber used. Usually it is either 6mm (¼in), 8mm (³⁄₁₆in), 10mm (³⁄₈in) or 12mm (½in).

Due to either size or intricate shape, our projects will only require 3mm (⅛in) or 6mm (¼in) legs. The latter may be bought already made, usually in 25mm (1in) or 30mm (1³⁄₁₆in) lengths, fluted and with their ends chamfered. The former you will need to make yourself, scoring your own flutes with a sharp implement such as an awl or knife. These flutes alleviate the hole pressure when gluing and prevent the timber from splitting.

Accurate marking out of where the dowel holes are to be drilled is vital. When using the 6mm (¼in) dowel pegs, the dowel centre points may be used as an aid (see **Fig 3.8**). Simply insert them into previously drilled dowel holes in one workpiece. Then push this workpiece against the other in the desired position. When taken apart, small indentations will be left on the other workpiece. These indicate the centres of the dowel holes to be drilled.

## Sharpness

The degree of sharpness of your tools with cutting edges is vital. Whether you are new to woodwork or not, you have probably heard the phrase 'Blunt tools are dangerous'. This is absolutely true.

*Fig 3.8*
**Wood twist bit and centre points.**

Sharp, well-maintained tools save time, trouble and accidents.

A cutting tool with a blunt edge will require a greater force in order to make it cut, and it will be more likely to deflect away from (or in the case of a hand plane, skim over the surface of) the workpiece.

Whole books have been written on the sharpening of tools, and it would be impossible for us to give full instructions of how to undertake all sharpening tasks in this brief section.

There are many places, such as saw sharpening specialists, that will sharpen and, if necessary, regrind the cutting edges of your tools. Your local commercial telephone book should have a list. Failing that, your local independent tool/hardware store will often know of someone who can do this service for you if you do not wish to do it yourself.

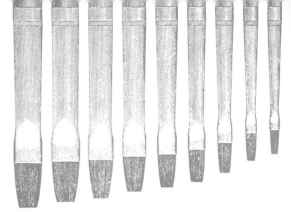

FOUR

# Painting & Finishing

This is the area in which you can really let your imagination run wild! You could finish the toys in a similar way to the ones we chose to show in this book, although using your own colour schemes and adding little personal touches really 'makes' a toy.

Children really appreciate a toy that has been personalized just for them. For example, this could be something as straightforward as putting the child's name, address and a fictitious haulage company name on the cab of the 18-Wheeler Lorry.

You could rename Chris Clown's Crazy Car using the child's name. Do try to keep it humorous – Brenda's Blinking Blundering Banger, or William's Wonderful Wonky Wonder!

Good stationers and some toy shops stock a range of transfers and stickers that can be used to decorate the toys. Also, most hardware and decorating shops sell sticky-backed plastic sheets in various colours, enabling you to make some designs of your own.

The design and style of some stickers or transfers may influence the whole colour scheme and theme of the toy.

Remember that transfers may need one or two coats of varnish to protect them.

Do not be afraid to experiment with colour. It is said that, under the right conditions, it is possible for someone with good eyesight to be able to detect up to 10 million different colours!

Understandably, most suppliers tend not to stock paint colours in such a range, so have a go at mixing and matching. An old white plate

serves as an excellent palette and may be cleaned easily and re-used.

Before applying paint, make absolutely sure that the workpiece surface is as clean and sound as possible. It is nigh on impossible to achieve a good finish if you do not prepare thoroughly first.

Ensure that the environment you choose for painting in is well-ventilated, warm, tidy and as clean and dust free as possible. A good light source is also essential, daylight being best.

Take your time when applying a finish. Quite often painting and, generally, finishing a project takes longer than the actual construction. It may be a bit of an old chestnut, but the adage, 'several light coats of paint are far better than one or two heavy ones', is on the whole true. After all, the overall effect and appeal of a design is largely influenced by the colour scheme and quality of finish.

When painting a decorative symbol or shape, try to paint boldly and with confidence. You will find you make less mistakes this way than when you are nervous – a tense hand will make the painting of flowing, even lines difficult.

Keeping your paint at the right consistency will help. If a paint pot has been in use for a while, and has been opened and closed frequently, the paint will invariably be too thick. Simply thin the paint with water or the appropriate solvent to the required viscosity.

Before finishing a project, think about how you will store the workpieces while their freshly painted surfaces are drying. You may find that you will have to make a few jigs or holding devices. These need not be elaborate. A few nails or dowel rods partly set into a length of timber and clamped to a table will act as a hanger for a multitude of items. Often, you will be able to use a drying jig many times for various projects.

Whatever paint, varnish or colouring medium you choose to use, make absolutely sure it is safe for children's toys. Many are, nowadays, but if you are unsure contact the manufacturers. They are usually pleased to advise you on their product.

Try to relax and enjoy finishing your toys. After all, you will have lavished time and care in their making. Quite often painting is forgiving. If you make a mistake you can usually paint over it later.

## Materials, techniques and tips

### Paint

There is a vast array of paints available, but we will concentrate on the two most common types used for toys.

Acrylic paint
The type that is convenient to use is Humbrol's Acrylic Colour. A wide range of colours is readily available in 12ml and 30ml sizes. It is water based, quick drying and easy to apply. All the colours are intermixable, and brushes may be cleaned with water. Most colours are available in matt and gloss.
Acrylic varnish and some useful metallic colours are also available.

Modelling enamels
Humbrol produces an excellent range of this non-toxic, oil-based paint, available in both matt and gloss finishes. They come in conveniently sized tins such as 14ml and 50ml.

All the colours are intermixable and fairly robust: they resist steam, boiling water, salt water, fumes, oil and dirt. Hopefully your toys will not be subjected to such elements and substances!

### Brushes

There is a wide range of brushes available. The sizes, styles and make you decide to use is a matter of personal preference. You may find one type of brush used for a certain job suits one person, but not another. So buy brushes that you feel comfortable with.

A useful tip if you find some fine brush handles too thin is to wrap adhesive tape around the handle until you achieve a more comfortable thickness.

When using new brushes for the first time, you may find it advantageous to clean them first. This will not only ensure that they are clean for use, it will also take away the odd loose hair or two which may otherwise spoil the painted finish.

Whatever brushes you choose to use, always try to ensure they are of good quality. It is false economy to buy cheap brushes – they will not last, and a satisfactory finish will be harder to achieve.

### Varnish

The varnish that we need concern ourselves with is available in two categories: polyurethane and acrylic.

Polyurethane varnish is a synthetic resin type that may be thinned with white spirit. Acrylic varnish may be thinned with water.

Both types are available in matt, satin and gloss finishes. Gloss varnish offers greater protection than matt or satin. If you prefer these latter finishes, use a gloss varnish for the first few coats, followed by matt or satin for the last one or two coats.

Both have various advantages and disadvantages over the other. Personal preference will determine which to use.

Applying varnish
Whatever type of varnish you choose to use, apply it with a good-quality, clean soft-bristled brush. Do not overload the brush and do not wipe it on the rim of the can. Wiping the brush on the rim of the can will create small air bubbles that will transfer to the surface of the workpiece.

On large flat areas, spread the varnish evenly in different directions, finishing with light 'laying off' strokes in the direction of the wood grain. Do this in small sections at a time.

When varnishing near an edge, brush towards it to prevent any surplus running down the sides.

Between coats, lightly sand away any dust particles or imperfections with a very fine grade of abrasive paper and/or 0000-grade wire wool.

**Velour**

Self-adhesive green velour, with its nylon pile,

provides an excellent covering material for the bases of some of the toys. It is also ideal for imitating grass, as in Classic Racing.

It is readily available in roll or sheet form from most hardware stores and hobbyist suppliers

## Dolls' house cladding paper

Available from hobbyist suppliers in a variety of colours and effects, this paper can be a very useful finishing material. For example, it could be used in Loader's Garage and Arthur's Tower.

FIVE

# Arthur's Tower

**T**oy castles are always popular with children, whether they are used for battles, storytelling or as ornaments. Many are, however, big and bulky, making storage space in smaller rooms a problem. Also, the towers of many toy castles, if they have any at all, are often inadequate and frustrating as toy soldiers and figures can rarely be placed inside them. Thus many toy castles are visually appealing but have limited play value for children and present storage problems to parents.

In designing Arthur's Tower we have attempted to solve these problems. The tower is freestanding, has no base and takes up only a small area of ground space (242 × 196mm (9½ × 7¾in)). This enables it to be stored on a bedroom/playroom shelf when not in use. The outer walls of the tower slot together so that when not in use they may be dismantled and stored easily.

To provide easy access to the many internal rooms, balconies and walkways, the back and the roof of the tower are removable. When not in use, toy soldiers/figures may be stored securely in the rooms.

If a castle, rather than just the tower, is desired, then the slot-together surrounding walls can be made.

Arthur's Tower has been designed to be used with toy knights in the Britain's (Petite) Ltd range. Britain's make an excellent range of mounted and foot figures (and even the odd dragon or two!).

**Good luck!** The adventure begins here!

## CUTTING LIST

**Tower** (all birch plywood)

| | |
|---|---|
| Inner front wall: | 550 x 150 x 6mm |
| | ($21^{21}/_{32}$ x $5^7/_8$ x $^1/_4$in) |
| Inner side wall (2): | 550 x 144 x 6mm |
| | ($21^{21}/_{32}$ x $5^{11}/_{16}$ x $^1/_4$in) |
| Outer base front wall: | 242 x 162 x 6mm |
| | ($9^1/_2$ x $6^3/_8$ x $^1/_4$in) |
| Outer base side wall (2): | 190 x 162 x 6mm |
| | ($7^1/_2$ x $6^3/_8$ x $^1/_4$in) |
| Front balcony wall: | 242 x 62 x 6mm |
| | ($9^1/_2$ x $2^7/_{16}$ x $^1/_4$in) |
| Back wall: | 547 x 230 x 6mm |
| | ($21^9/_{16}$ x $9^1/_{16}$ x $^1/_4$in) |
| Side balcony wall (2): | 190 x 62 x 6mm |
| | ($7^1/_2$ x $2^7/_{16}$ x $^1/_4$in) |
| Bottom walkway: | 230 x 190 x 12mm |
| | ($9^1/_{16}$ x $7^1/_2$ x $^1/_2$in) |
| Balcony walkway: | 230 x 190 x 12mm |
| | ($9^1/_{16}$ x $7^1/_2$ x $^1/_2$in) |
| First floor: | 138 x 138 x 12mm |
| | ($5^7/_{16}$ x $5^7/_{16}$ x $^1/_2$in) |
| Other floors (3): | 144 x 138 x 12mm |
| | ($5^{11}/_{16}$ x $5^7/_{16}$ x $^1/_2$in) |
| Underside roof section: | 144 x 138 x 3mm |
| | ($5^{11}/_{16}$ x $5^7/_{16}$ x $^1/_8$in) |
| Base roof section: | 150 x 150 x 6mm |
| | ($5^7/_8$ x $5^7/_8$ x $^1/_4$in) |
| Top roof section: | 120 x 120 x 18mm |
| | ($4^3/_4$ x $4^3/_4$ x $^3/_4$in) |

**Surrounding Tower Walls** (all birch plywood, *except where otherwise noted*)

| | | |
|---|---|---|
| Front main wall: | | 564 x 162 x 6mm |
| | | ($22^3/_{16}$ x $6^3/_8$ x $^1/_4$in) |
| Back wall: | | 564 x 120 x 6mm |
| | | ($22^3/_{16}$ x $4^3/_4$ x $^1/_4$in) |
| Side wall (2): | | 516 x 120 x 6mm |
| | | ($20^5/_{16}$ x $4^3/_4$ x $^1/_4$in) |
| Walkways: | Front: | 144 x 25 x 12mm |
| | | ($5^{11}/_{16}$ x 1 x $^1/_2$in) |
| | Front (2): | 177 x 25 x 12mm |
| | | ($6^{15}/_{16}$ x 1 x $^1/_2$in) |
| | Back: | 532 x 25 x 12mm |
| | | ($20^{15}/_{16}$ x 1 x $^1/_2$in) |
| | Sides (2): | 484 x 25 x 12mm |
| | | ($19^1/_{16}$ x 1 x $^1/_2$in) |
| Steps (2): | | 45 x 30 x 25mm |
| | | ($1^3/_4$ x $1^3/_{16}$ x 1in) |

**Flagpole**
154 x 5mm ($6^1/_{16}$ x $^3/_{16}$in) diameter dowel
25mm (*1in*) diameter wooden bead
10mm (*$^3/_8$in*) diameter wooden bead

**Miscellaneous**
(2) 31mm (*$1^1/_4$in*) butterfly hinges
(4) 16mm (*$^5/_8$in*) brass butt hinges
(4) decorative upholstery nails (for door handles)
(4) turnbuttons

## Construction

### Castellations

Due to the size and scale of the tower, the dimensions of the castellations vary, albeit slightly, between the front and side wall sections. However, their vertical length remains constant at 16mm ($^5/_8$in). The horizontal lengths are all approximately 16mm ($^5/_8$in) (usually a fraction over). At the end of this section a list of the exact horizontal lengths is given (not on the drawings for reasons of clarity).

**Tip** To ensure correct dimensions it is best to mark the horizontal length of the castellations by dividing the width of the workpiece in the manner shown in the section entitled 'Dividing A Line' found on page 10.

## Tower

Main inner walls
Mark and cut out the front and side inner walls of the tower (see **Fig 5.1**). The arched door at the bottom of the front inner walls is drawn using French curves. Draw the curve to the shape you wish. Fix the front wall onto the edges of the side walls with glue and moulding pins. This will produce the inner frame of the tower, the dimensions of which are 550 x 150 x 150mm ($21^5/_8$ x $5^7/_8$ x $5^7/_8$in).

Floors
Mark, cut out and fit all the floors of the rooms into the positions shown in Fig 5.2 using glue and moulding pins. Ensure that the smaller of the four floors is used for the first floor (see **Fig 5.3**).

Outer walls
Mark and cut out all the outer front and side

Fig 5.1
**Inner front wall** (a) **and inner side walls** (b).

A

B

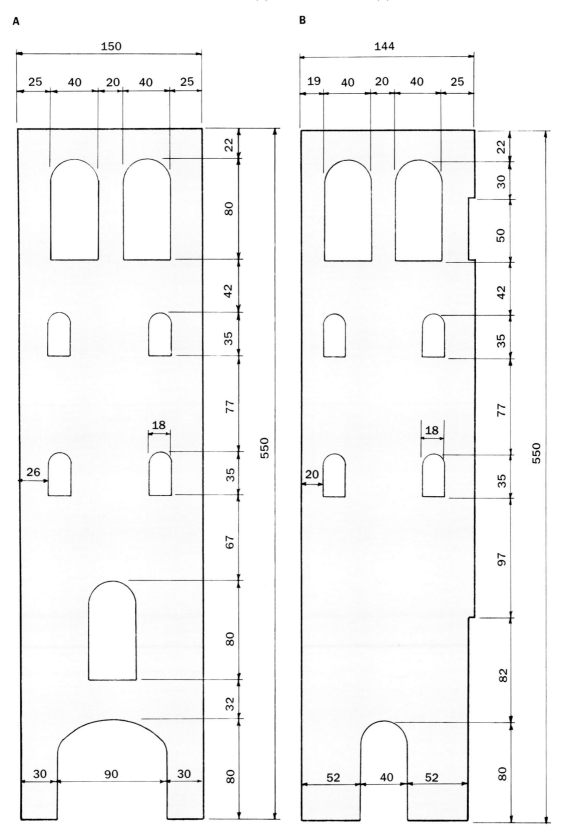

base walls (see **Fig 5.4**). If you carefully cut out the profile of the front doorway you will be able to use the waste piece to make the doors. Do this by marking and then cutting a central vertical dividing line.

Fix the front outer wall onto the edges of the side outer walls with glue and moulding pins. When assembled, the dimensions of this section should be 242 x 196 x 162mm (9⁹⁄₁₆ x 7¾ x 6⅜in).

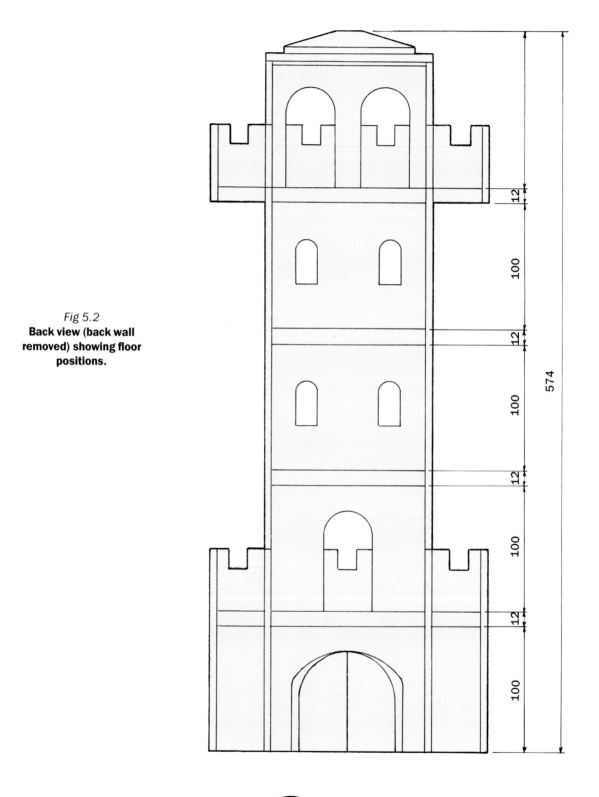

Fig 5.2
**Back view (back wall removed) showing floor positions.**

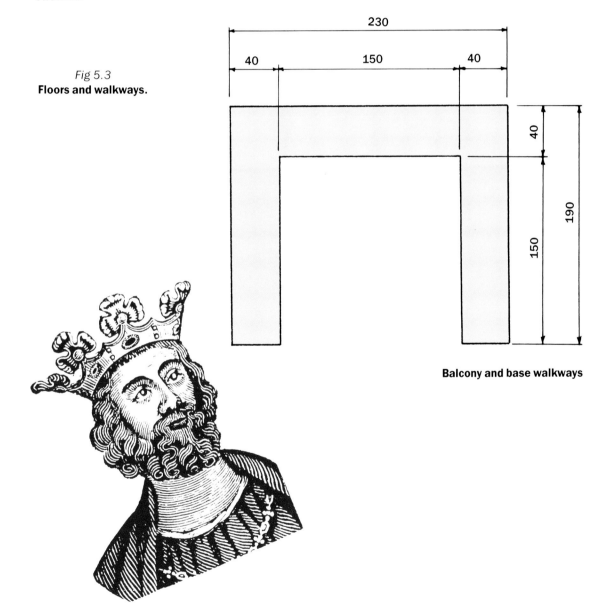

138

138

**First floor**

144

138

**Other floors**

*Fig 5.3*
**Floors and walkways.**

230

40    150    40

40

190

150

**Balcony and base walkways**

**Walkways**

Fix the walkway (see **Fig 5.3**) into position on the outer wall using glue and pins. The top surface of the walkway should be 50mm (2in) down from the top of the castellations and must be at the same height as the bottom of the door in the front inner wall (see **Fig 5.2**). Glue the outer walls and walkway to the inner section of the tower. If careful measuring and cutting has been undertaken it should slot into position easily. Use cramps if necessary to hold them in position until the glue has set.

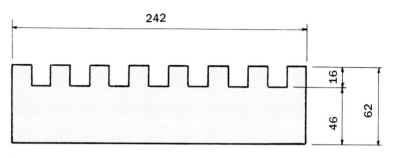

**Balcony front wall**

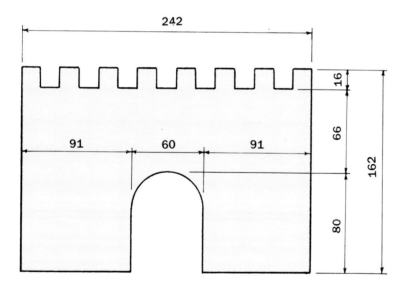

**Base front wall**

*Fig 5.4*
**Balcony and base walls.**

Balcony

Glue and pin the walkways to the top balcony walls (see **Fig 5.4**). Glue, and cramp if necessary, the balcony into position on the inner section of the tower. The top of the walkway should be flush with the top floor of the tower (see **Fig 5.2**).

Underneath the balcony we added 20mm ($1^3/_{16}$in) scotia moulding for decoration, but you could use any type that appeals to you, or omit it altogether.

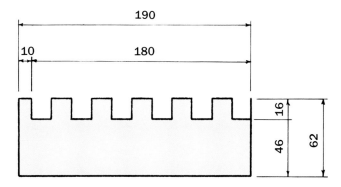

**Balcony side wall**

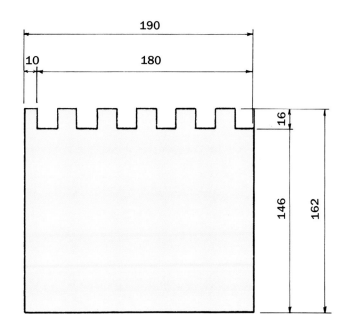

**Base side wall**

## Roof

Glue the 3mm (⅛in) plywood to the 6mm (¼in) plywood base. Fig 5.5 shows the correct position. The top of the roof is made from a piece of 18mm (¾in) plywood. Shape the top slopes of the roof with a block plane. Make sure that the workpiece is secured tightly in a vice when doing this. Drill a 5mm (³⁄₁₆in) diameter hole in the top of the roof to a depth of 6mm (¼in).

Finally, glue the roof top to the roof base. Remember not to glue the roof section to the tower if you wish it to be removable during play.

## Flagpole

Construct the flagpole as shown in Fig 5.6. When drilling through the 25mm (1in) bead, and partway into the 10mm (⅜in) bead, ensure that these are held securely in a vice.

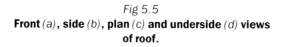

*Fig 5.5*
**Front** *(a)*, **side** *(b)*, **plan** *(c)* **and underside** *(d)* **views of roof.**

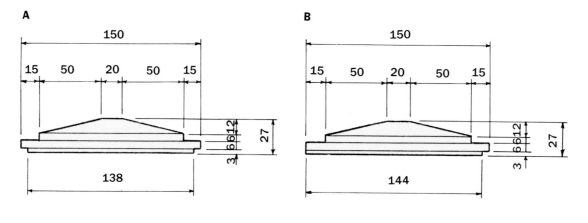

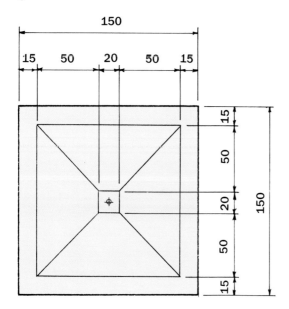

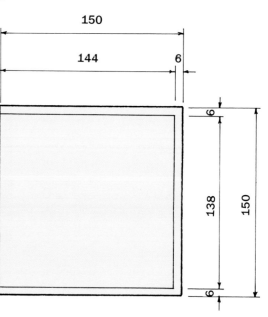

**Tip** A hand drill is easier to use than a power drill.

The flagpole should not be glued to the roof, as we recommend that it be removed when young children play with the tower.

Flag

Feel free to make the flag to your own design using the material of your choice. The one shown is made from paper and painted.

Tower back

Cut out the back wall profile, including the window (see **Fig 5.7**). Later, this window will act as a finger hole when the back wall needs to be removed. You may wish to add further

windows, but remember that it is unlikely that the wall will remain in position during use.

Ensure that the back wall does not fit too tightly, thus hindering easy removal.

To secure the back of the tower in place, turnbuttons (*used on picture frames*) are fixed to the back edges of the tower sides (see **Fig 5.8**).

## Surrounding tower walls

Cut out the profiles for the front, back and side walls (see **Figs 5.9–5.12**). Likewise, the

*Fig 5.6*
**The flagpole.**

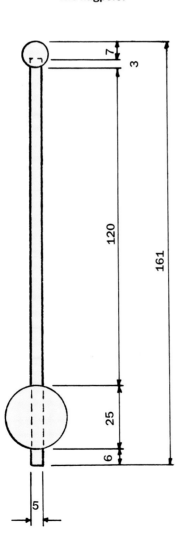

*Fig 5.7*
**The back wall.**

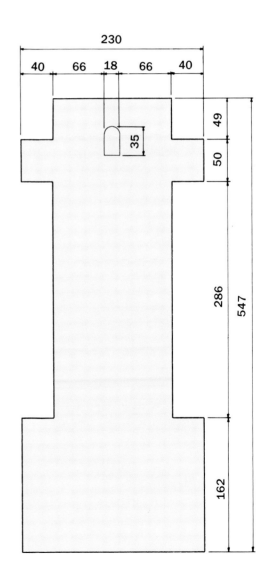

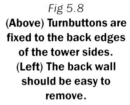

*Fig 5.8*
**(Above) Turnbuttons are fixed to the back edges of the tower sides. (Left) The back wall should be easy to remove.**

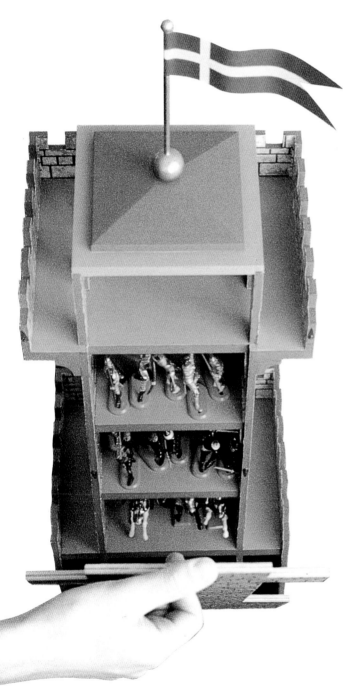

walkways (see **Fig 5.13**) and steps. The steps should ideally be cut from a suitable hardwood such as beech. A softwood could be used, but would not wear so well. When cutting the wall-joining slots, ensure that you allow for the thickness of either the covering paper or paint finish as, obviously, a tight fit will make it difficult to assemble and disassemble.

Before gluing and pinning the walkways into position, mitre the ends that will be next to the wall slots. This is to enable the walkway ends to butt together neatly when the walls are assembled.

The front wall doors are made in the same manner as the front doors of the tower.

*Fig 5.9*
**Front and back view of tower's front surrounding
wall.**

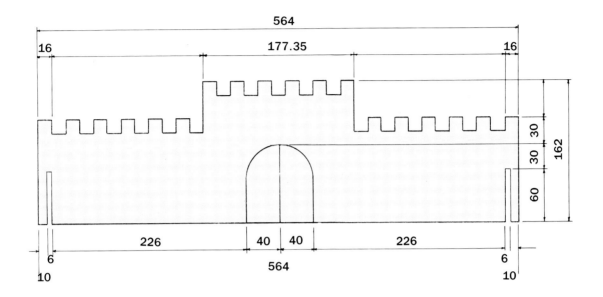

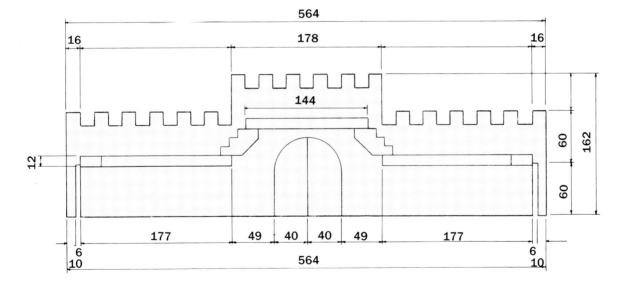

Fig 5.10
**The tower's four surrounding walls.**

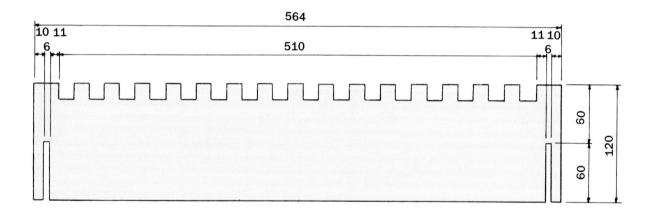

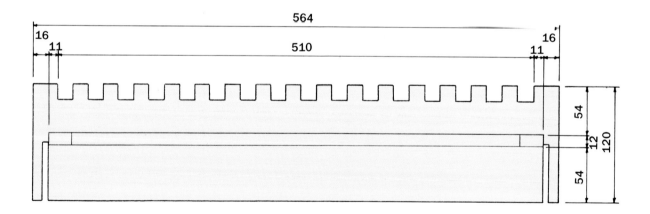

Fig 5.11
**Front and back view of tower's back surrounding
wall.**

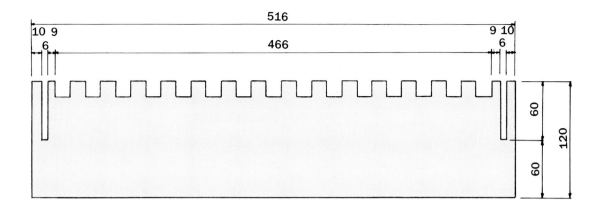

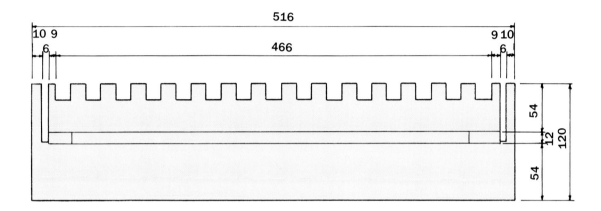

**Fig 5.12**
**Front and back view of side wall (tower's surrounding wall).**

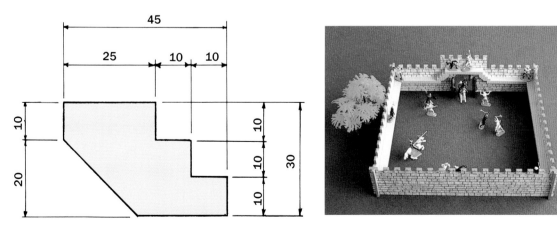

**Fig 5.13**
**Steps adjoining lower and higher walkways.**

**Fig 5.14**
**The surrounding walls in place.**

## Finishing the tower and surrounding walls

The tower can be finished to suit your own particular taste – either painted and/or papered with brick print paper (available from hobbyist suppliers). If you cover it with paper, paint all edges and the window sides prior to applying the paper.

*Fig 5.15*
**Arthur's Tower in use.**

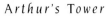

## Alternatives

The dimensions and scale of the tower and the surrounding walls could be altered to suit your own requirements. Also, there are various construction and play alternatives. For example:

• For added play value, the tower may be placed and used separately from the surrounding walls, thus creating two play castles – the walled surround now becoming a fort or castle in its own right.

• A less ambitious and more economic alternative would be to construct the tower base walls only, with a solid piece being substituted for the walkway (made to the same external dimensions as the walkways). Cut the back wall the same height as the base walls. Cut castellations at the top, but do not cut out a window from it. As with the original tower, use turnbuttons to retain it.

Make the surrounding slot-together walls and place this around the new small tower. This new arrangement will create an economical play castle.

*Fig 5.16*
**Let battle commence.**

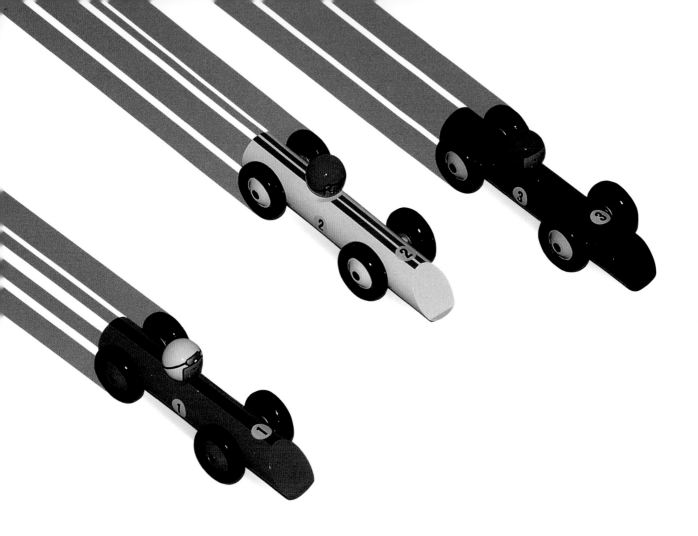

# SIX

# Broomstick Racers

As their name suggests, these simple yet effective toy cars have their main bodies made from a length of broomstick! Or, as is the case with the ones shown in the photographs, a rake handle. You may use whatever you choose, but it should not be under 25mm (1in) in diameter.

This project is very suitable for children to undertake, with, of course, adult supervision. Our nine-year-old nephew made one in an afternoon.

We have finished these racers in two different styles: the cars have either been simply coloured using thinned acrylic paint, or elaborately painted, making them ideal for use as decorations in a child's bedroom.

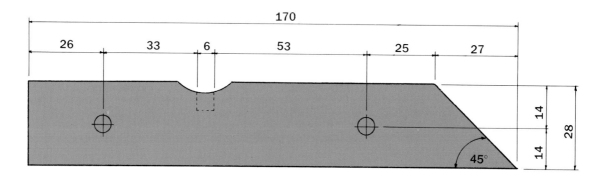

*Fig 6.1*
**Side view and dimensions for the car body.**

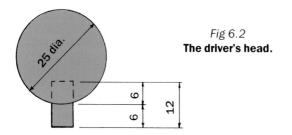

*Fig 6.2*
**The driver's head.**

## MATERIALS LIST

Length of broomstick or 25mm (1in)
  diameter dowel rod
Length of 6mm (¼in) diameter
  dowel rod
38mm (1½in) diameter ready-made
  wood wheels
25mm (1in) wood balls or beads

## Construction

Sand smooth the length of broomstick (or
dowel).

Cut one end square (see **Fig 6.1**). 70mm
(6¹¹/₁₆in) along from this cut end make a
second cut at 45°. This may be done using
either a mitre jig or a mitre box (see **Fig 2.9
on page 9**). The bottom edge of the mitred
cut may be flattened if required to give a
snub-nosed effect. Use a sanding block to do
this. Sand the cuts smooth.

Drill the axle holes and the hole that will later
receive the driver's neck – this should be to a
depth of 6mm (¼in). Note that the axle holes
will need to be of a diameter size that will
enable the axles to turn freely, whereas the
driver's neck (connecting dowel) should fit
snugly.

The cockpit depression is made by wrapping
abrasive paper around a piece of dowel of the
same diameter as the car body and, using this
as a sanding block, sanding the shape of the
cockpit out of the car body. Start with a coarse
grade of abrasive paper and work
progressively down to a fine one. The size of
the cockpit is entirely up to you.

Drill the axle holes in each wheel to a size that
will ensure a snug fit.

Cut the driver's neck from 6mm (¼in) dowel
rod 12mm (½in) in length (see **Fig 6.2**).

In the 25mm (1in) wood ball/bead, which is to
be used as the driver's head, drill a 6mm (¼in)
deep hole to snugly receive the neck dowel.
Glue the neck into the head.

## Finishing & assembly

Paint/stain all the parts of the car before final
assembly.

**Tip**  When colouring or staining the wheels
with thinned acrylic paint, mark around the
inside of the wheel tyre with a black Biro pen.
This will help prevent the paint or stain from
spreading from the wheel hub to the tyre
section.

When the finishing is complete, measure and
cut the two axles. Pass the axles through the
axle holes and glue the wheels to the ends of
the axles (see **Fig 6.3**).

Finally, glue the head into position in the
cockpit.

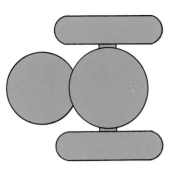

*Fig 6.4*
**Broomstick racers with a simple stained finish.**

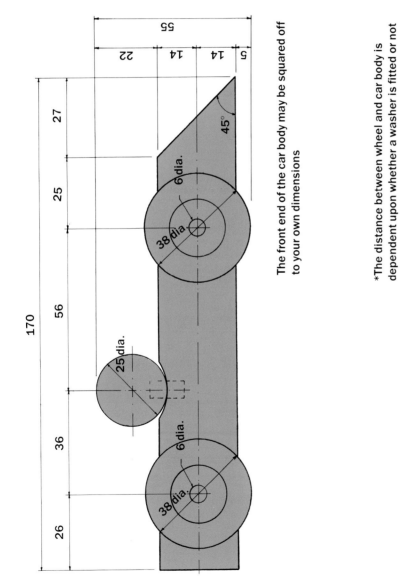

The front end of the car body may be squared off to your own dimensions

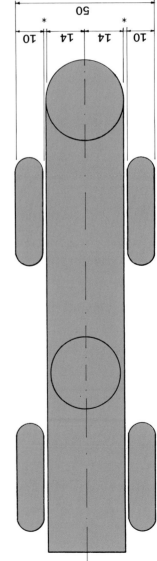

*The distance between wheel and car body is dependent upon whether a washer is fitted or not

*Fig 6.3*
**Side, rear and plan views.**

SEVEN

# Butterfly Mobile

**H**ung from a ceiling, this colourful toy will provide interest and stimulation for babies and young children. A gentle spin of the hanging disc or a slight breeze will make the butterflies flutter and dance!

### CUTTING LIST

Butterflies: various scraps of 3mm (⅛in) plywood
Lengths of string/cord for hanging
Hanging disc: 203mm (8in) diameter disc of 3mm (⅛in) plywood

## Construction

### Butterflies

Transfer the butterfly profiles (see **Fig 7.1**) to the plywood and cut out using a fretsaw.

Drill a 2mm (³⁄₃₂in) hole centrally in the head of each butterfly.

Paint all the butterflies.

### Hanging disc

Set a compass to a 100mm (4in) radius and draw the 200mm (8in) diameter disc onto the plywood (see **Fig 7.2**).

Next, set the compass to draw a circle of 190mm (7½in) diameter – the butterfly hanging holes will be marked on the circumference of this circle.

Set the compass to mark an 80mm (3⁵⁄₃₂in) diameter circle – the mobile's hanging holes will be positioned around the circumference of this circle.

Using a protractor, divide the disc into 36° segments from its central point. Using an awl, lightly mark every other point where the segment lines cross the 190mm (7½in) diameter circle (butterfly holes).

Likewise, do the same with the smaller inner circle, but this time mark every other hole between the ones marked on the outer circle (see **Fig 7.2**).

Fig 7.1
**Actual size butterfly plans.**

Drill all the marked holes, including the disc's centre, with a 2mm (³⁄₃₂in) drill bit.

## Final assembly

Attach the butterflies to the disc with thread, ensuring that they all hang at different heights.

Use a stronger thread/cord to hang the mobile to the ceiling.

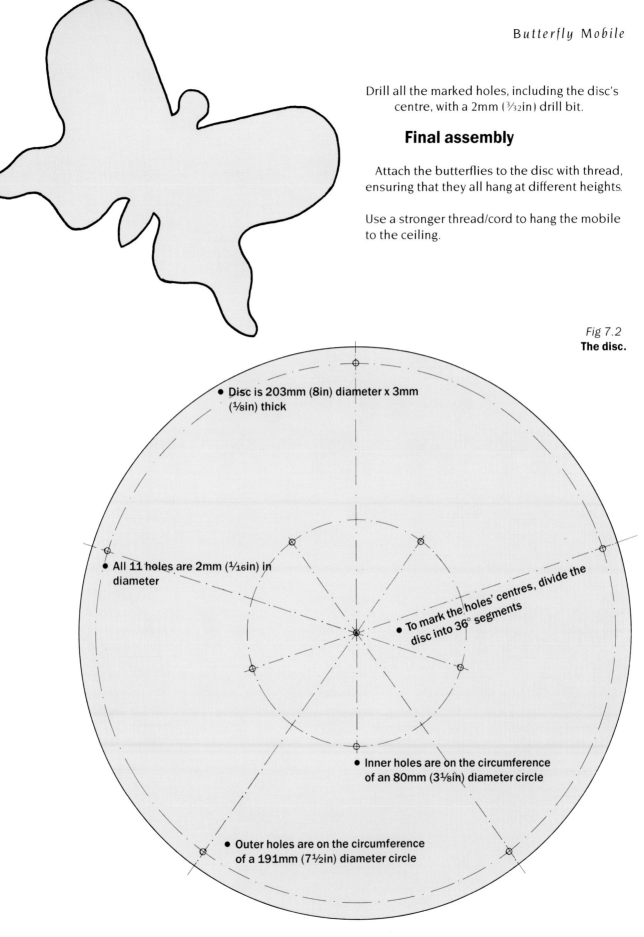

*Fig 7.2*
**The disc.**

- Disc is 203mm (8in) diameter x 3mm (⅛in) thick

- All 11 holes are 2mm (¹⁄₁₆in) in diameter

- To mark the holes' centres, divide the disc into 36° segments

- Inner holes are on the circumference of an 80mm (3⅛in) diameter circle

- Outer holes are on the circumference of a 191mm (7½in) diameter circle

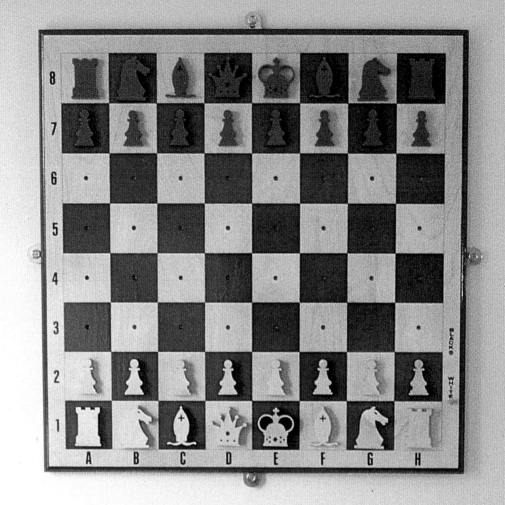

E I G H T

# Wall-mounted Chessboard

Chess is an ever popular game. Children and adult chess fans alike will love to play a game on this large board. The large squares, easily recognizable chessmen and the rank-and-file numbering and lettering make it an ideal aid in teaching the game to novices.

One of its main advantages is that it is wall mounted, so storing it is no problem. A small shelf could be fixed underneath upon which to place captured pieces.

It is possible to play a game on this board over several days. For example, hung on a wall in the hall, moves may be made when a player passes by. To keep track of whose turn it is, a turn/move indicator is situated at the bottom right-hand side of the board. This consists of two peg holes (one marked WHITE, the other BLACK) and a peg. When a player has made a move, he places the peg into his opponent's colour peg pole, thus indicating that it is the opponent's move next.

The chessmen are fretsawed from 12mm (½in) birch plywood. While it is quite possible to cut these out using a hand-held fretsaw (much care, attention and patience required!), it is advisable to use a powered fretsaw if at all possible.

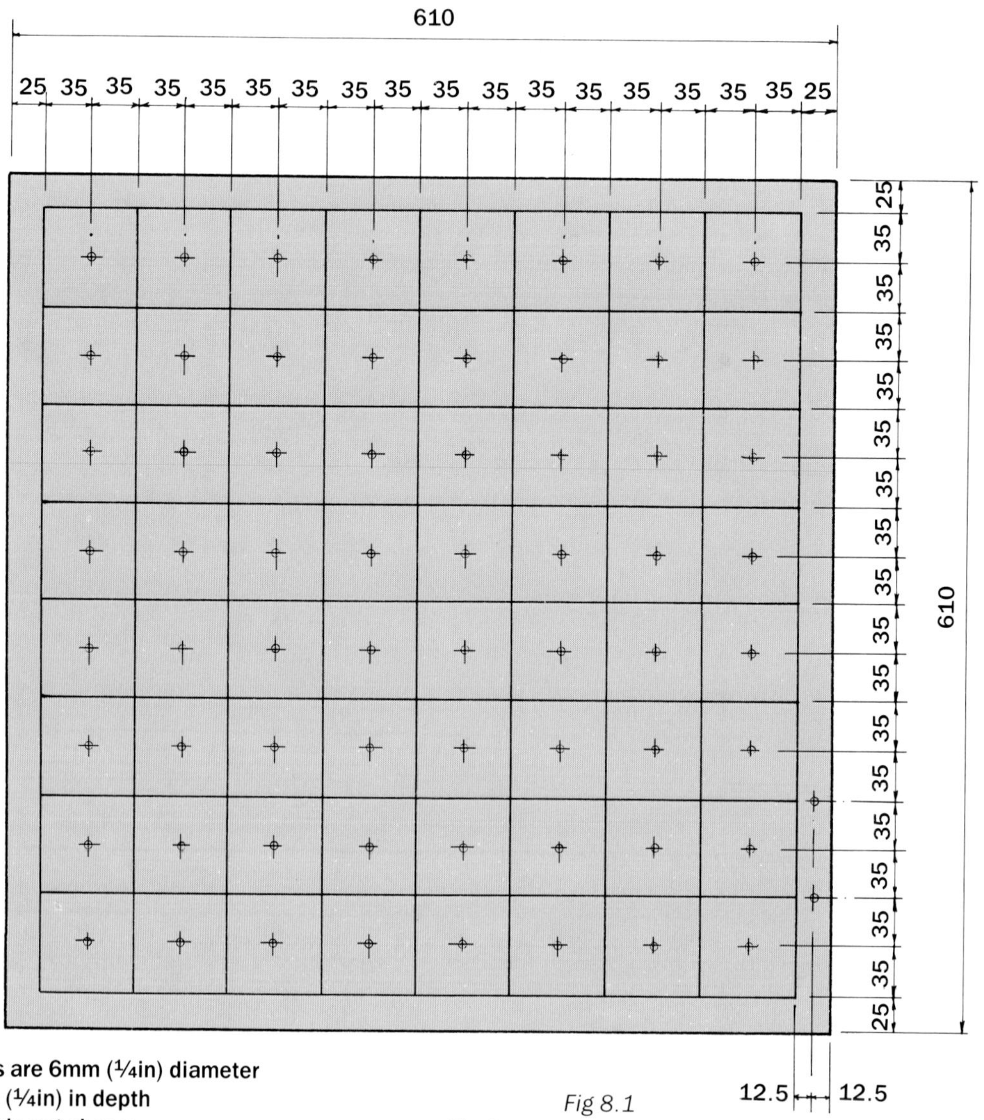

610

25 | 35 | 35 | 35 | 35 | 35 | 35 | 35 | 35 | 35 | 35 | 35 | 35 | 35 | 35 | 35 | 35 | 25

25 35 35 35 35 35 35 35 35 35 35 35 35 35 35 35 35 25

610

*Fig 8.1*
**The layout of the chessboard.**

12.5 — 12.5

- Peg holes are 6mm (¼in) diameter and 6mm (¼in) in depth
- Edging strip not shown

---

### CUTTING LIST

Board: 610 x 610 x 12mm (*24 x 24 x ½in*)
   birch plywood
Chessmen: various scraps of 12mm (*½in*)
   birch plywood

**Miscellaneous**
Approximately 2,440mm (*96in*) suitable
   moulding or strip wood for edging
(2) 30 x 6mm (*1³/₁₆ x ¼in*) diameter joining
   dowels
(32) 12 x 6mm (*½ x ¼in*) diameter dowels
(4) large mirror plates and screws
(4) rubber buffers
Dry rub-down letters and numbers

## Construction

### The board

After cutting out the board, plane the edges square, preferably using a block plane.

Then sand smooth the top surface of the board. Using a sharp 2H pencil and a 600mm (2ft) rule, lightly mark out the layout of the chessboard (see **Fig 8.1**).

Drill the 64 peg holes in the centre of each square and the two turn/move indicator peg holes, all to the depth of 6mm (¼in).

**Tip** Prior to drilling, ensure that the dowel pegs that you intend to use will fit easily, but not loosely, in the hole produced by your chosen drill bit. Test on a scrap piece of 12mm (½in) plywood first.

Using a Biro and rule, mark over the pencil layout lines. It is better to use two or three light strokes of the pen when marking each line than one heavy one. Wipe the pen nib after each stroke. These techniques will help you to produce even, clean and bold lines. Use a Biro whose ink will match the colour of the 32 'black' squares. Erase any remaining pencil lines.

Seal all the 'white' squares and the border with gloss polyurethane varnish. When the varnish is dry, the 'black' squares may be coloured. We used a blue acrylic paint, which was thinned to produce a water stain. Use a palette (an old white plate, or even a clean, white margarine tub lid) to thin a little of the paint at a time.

Test your colouring medium on a scrap piece of plywood before applying it to your chessboard. When doing this you will notice that the colour will tend to 'creep' along the direction of the grain. It is for this reason you have sealed the 'white' squares with varnish. The seal, coupled with the Biroed lines, should prevent any creep when applying thinned acrylic colour. However, be especially careful if you wish to use a proprietary brand of woodshade stain (either water or spirit based), as these tend to penetrate the wood grain and creep at a faster rate.

When the colour is dry, varnish over the entire board.

If you wish to apply an edging strip to the board, do it now. We used 15 x 10mm (⅝ x ⅜in) glass beading. It is advisable to colour the edging before applying it. Glue and pin it into place and then touch up any areas where the colour has been removed.

Apply two coats of varnish to the entire board, sanding lightly between coats.

Apply the words 'BLACK' and 'WHITE' and the rank-and-file letters and numbers. We used 18mm (¾in) elongated letters and numbers for the rank and file and 5mm (³⁄₁₆in) letters for the words 'BLACK' and 'WHITE'.

Give the entire chessboard a further two or three coats of varnish.

Fix the four large brass mirror plates to the back of the board with screws. Situate one, with the wall-mounting screw hole protruding, at the centre of each side. You will find that, if you use the same edging as us, the mirror plate will not fit flush to the back of the board as the glass beading is thicker than the 12mm (½in) plywood. To remedy this, place washers between the mirror plate and the board.

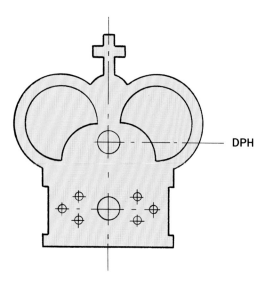

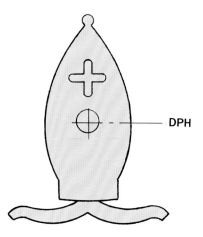

Large hole: 6mm (¼in) dia.
Small holes: 2mm (³⁄₃₂in) dia.

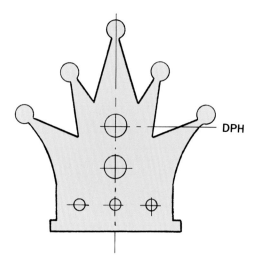

Large hole: 6mm (¼in) dia.
Small hole: 3mm (⅛in) dia.

*Fig 8.2*
**The chessmen. 'DPH' means that the dowel peg-hole has been drilled halfway.**

## The chessmen

Transfer the images of the chesspieces to 12mm (½in) birch plywood (see **Fig 8.2**).

Drill peg holes to a depth of 6mm (¼in) and a diameter of 6mm (¼in) in each piece. Also drill any decorative holes before cutting out the pieces.

The decorative cross on each bishop is made by drilling each end with a 2mm (³⁄₃₂in) drill bit, placing a fretsaw blade through one of the holes and then cutting along each line of the cross.

Similarly, the knight's eye is first drilled using a 3mm (⅛in) drill bit and then fretsawed to shape.

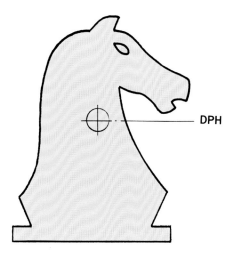

DPH

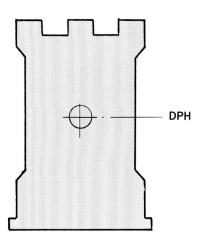

DPH

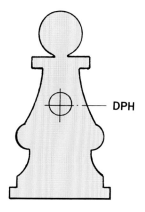

DPH

When you have fretsawed out all the pieces, sand them smooth.

Colour or stain the 'black' chessmen (we used a thinned red acrylic paint) and leave the 'white' pieces natural. Varnish all the pieces.

When the varnish is dry fix in the attaching pegs.

# NINE

# Chris Clown's Crazy Car

*This pull-along action toy comes to you straight from the circus.*

*As they drive along, Chris and his car do the craziest things: the bonnet and boot of the car open and bang closed, and Chris's neck grows tall and then shrinks!*

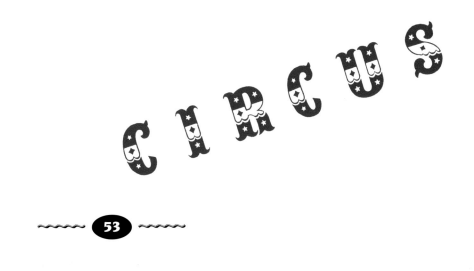

## CUTTING LIST

*(All birch plywood)*

| | |
|---|---|
| Car side (2): | 240 x 60 x 2mm |
| | ($9\frac{1}{2}$ x $2\frac{3}{8}$ x $\frac{1}{4}$in) |
| Car top: | 212 x 66 x 6mm |
| | ($8\frac{3}{8}$ x $2\frac{9}{16}$ x $\frac{1}{4}$in) |
| Car front: | 64 x 54 x 12mm |
| | ($2\frac{1}{2}$ x $2\frac{1}{8}$ x $\frac{1}{2}$in) |
| Car back: | 64 x 36 x 12mm |
| | ($2\frac{1}{2}$ x $1\frac{7}{16}$ x $\frac{1}{2}$in) |
| Bonnet/Boot retainer (2): | 78 x 16 x 6mm |
| | ($3\frac{1}{16}$ x $\frac{5}{8}$ x $\frac{1}{4}$in) |
| Windscreen: | 78 x 44 x 6mm |
| | ($3\frac{1}{16}$ x $1\frac{3}{4}$ x $\frac{1}{4}$in) |
| Boot top piece: | 78 x 52 x 6mm |
| | ($3\frac{1}{16}$ x $2\frac{1}{16}$ x $\frac{1}{4}$in) |
| Boot back piece: | 66 x 30 x 3mm |
| | ($6\frac{9}{16}$ x $1\frac{3}{16}$ x $\frac{1}{8}$in) |
| Bonnet: | 102 x 60 x 6mm |
| | ($4\frac{1}{16}$ x $2\frac{3}{8}$ x $\frac{1}{4}$in) |
| Wing (2): | 102 x 12 x 6mm |
| | ($4\frac{1}{16}$ x $\frac{1}{2}$ x $\frac{1}{4}$in) |
| Follower connecting strip (2): | 170 x 10 x 3mm |
| | ($6\frac{11}{16}$ x $\frac{3}{8}$ x $\frac{1}{8}$in) |

| | |
|---|---|
| Overhead cam follower (2): | 40 x 30 x 12mm |
| | ($1\frac{19}{32}$ x $1\frac{3}{16}$ x $\frac{1}{2}$in) |
| Follower connected to head: | 62 x 25 x 3mm |
| | ($2\frac{7}{16}$ x 1 x $\frac{1}{8}$in) |
| Cam (2): | 26mm ($1\frac{1}{32}$in) |
| | diameter x 12mm |
| | ($\frac{1}{2}$in) thick |

**Miscellaneous**

25mm *(1in)* wooden bead for head
6mm – 10mm *($\frac{1}{4}$in – $\frac{3}{8}$in)* bead for nose
(5) 22mm *($\frac{7}{8}$in)* wood buttons
6mm *($\frac{1}{4}$in)* dowel rod
(4) 63mm *($2\frac{1}{2}$in)* wooden wheels
Small amount of 3mm *($\frac{1}{8}$in)* plywood for
   mouth
String/Cord
(4) 16mm *($\frac{5}{8}$in)* brass hinges and small
   screws
(8) No. 2 $\frac{3}{8}$in roundhead screws

## The mechanism

All this movement is controlled by a simple cam system (see **Fig 9.1**). In this instance the cam is a wheel with its axle hole drilled off-centre.

Attached to the centre of each wheel axle rod is a small cam which, when turned, raises and lowers an overhead axle follower (a small rectangle of ply with a peg attached to the top). Then the pegs situated above each follower push open and close the bonnet and boot.

The two axle followers are connected together by two loose fitted strips of 3mm ($\frac{1}{8}$in) plywood. Another follower connected to Chris Clown's head rests on these strips. When the car is driven along, the strips cause the follower to raise and lower Chris's head!

## Construction

Cut out all the components for Chris's car from birch plywood. The components are listed in the cutting list and illustrated in Figs 9.2–9.4. The assembly plan is shown in Fig 9.1.

## The main car body

The axles are made from 6mm ($\frac{1}{4}$in) ramin dowel. Drill the axle holes into the car sides with a drill bit that allows the axle rods to turn freely.

Assemble the sides of the car to the front and back pieces using pins and glue.

Prior to fitting the top piece, drill the holes for the pegs that will activate the bonnet, the boot and Chris's head. Again, drill these holes with a suitably sized drill bit that will allow free movement of the 6mm ($\frac{1}{4}$in) pegs.

**Note** Before drilling the hole for Chris's neck, make sure that the bead you use for his nose will not hit the windscreen frame when in use. If it looks likely that it will, you could either: set Chris's neck hole backwards slightly; use a smaller bead; or set his head facing slightly to one side when in position.

*Fig 9.1*
**The cams and followers, a positional guide.**

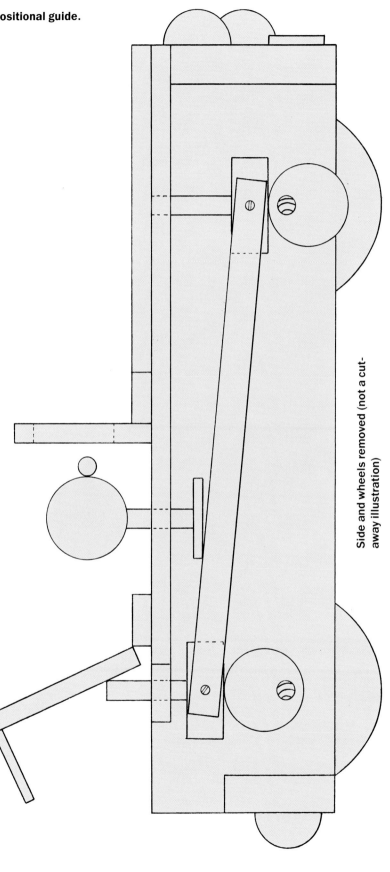

Side and wheels removed (not a cut-away illustration)

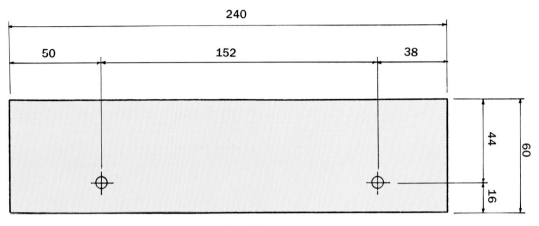

**Side (2)**

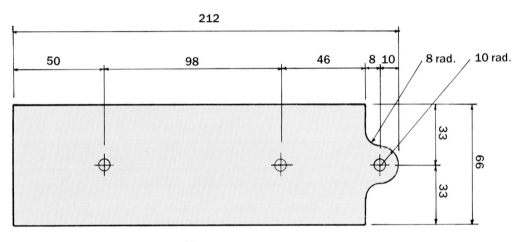

**Top**

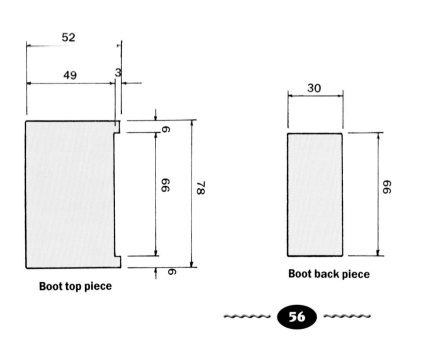

**Boot top piece**

**Boot back piece**

*Fig 9.2*
**Body parts of the car.**

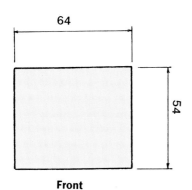

**Front**

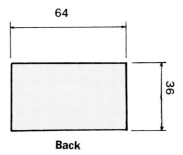

**Back**

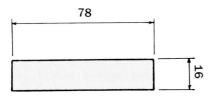

**Bonnet/boot retainer (2)**

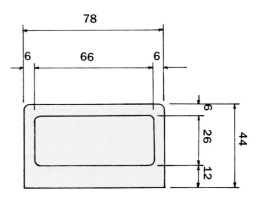

**Windscreen**

- The internal and top external corners of the windscreen are rounded to a 6mm (¼in) radius

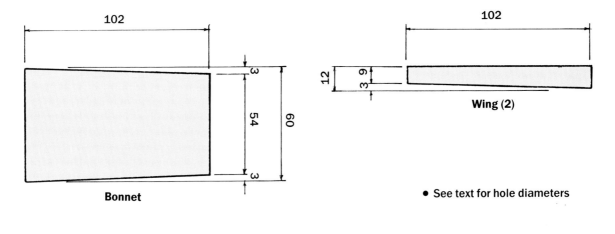

**Bonnet**

**Wing (2)**

- See text for hole diameters

Of course, you could add to the fun if you allow him to purposely 'bash' his nose as he travels along!

To the top of the car attach the bonnet's retaining strip, front wings, the boot's retaining strip and the windscreen. Glue and pins should suffice, but, for a stronger fit, you may wish to attach the windscreen using small (3mm (⅛in)) dowel joints.

Fix the tailpiece of the boot to its top. Then make sure that the bonnet and boot fit snugly into position. These should not fit too tightly as subsequent layers of paint may prevent them from opening easily.

Glue the 22mm (⅞in) diameter wood buttons for the eyes, nose and rear lights into position.

Drill a 3mm (⅛in) hole in the centre of the mouth of the car (see **Fig 9.3**). This will allow a fretsaw blade to pass through it, thus enabling you to cut out the centre 'smile' curve of the lips. With this done, glue the mouth into

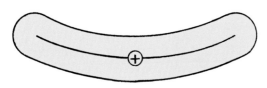

3mm (⅛in) thick
Hole size: 3.5 (⅛+in) dia.

Fig 9.3
**Pattern for the car's 'mouth'.**

position. When the glue has set again, drill a 3mm (⅛in) diameter hole through the mouth and right through the front of the car. This hole will later be used to attach a piece of cord to the car in order to pull it along. In this position it gives the impression that the car is holding the cord with its 'teeth'!

The body, bonnet and boot of the car may now be painted.

## The cam system

The cams are fretsawed from 12mm (½in) birch plywood (see **Fig 9.4**). Drill their axle holes first before cutting them out. Make sure that the size of the axle holes allows a firm and positive fit of the axle rods. Unlike the sides of the car, where some free movement is desirable, the cams have to be glued firmly to the axle rods later on, so you do not want a loose and free fit.

The axle cam followers have 6mm (¼in) dowels fitted centrally to their tops. Sink the dowel pegs halfway into the followers. At this stage, cut the dowel pegs slightly longer than you require (30mm (1³⁄₁₆in), approximately), as you will cut them to size when the car has been assembled.

The follower attached to Chris's head is cut from 3mm (⅛in) birch plywood. The 6mm (¼in) dowel peg (Chris's neck) is fitted centrally into it. In this instance the peg is fitted all the way through the follower but is flush on the bottom.

The strips which connect the front and back axle followers are attached to the sides of these followers with No 2. (⅜in) roundhead brass screws. These must not fit tightly and should allow free upward and downward movement of the followers. Before drilling the screw holes into the strips, make sure that the shank of the screw (but not the head) will fit easily through with the drill bit you intend to use.

## Wheels

Four 63mm (2½in) diameter wood wheels are used for the wheels of the car. Drill their axle holes so as to allow the axle rods a firm fit.

Then paint and decorate the wheels as desired.

Alternative
Instead of drilling the axle holes centrally, you may wish to offset them, thus making the car bump up and down or side to side. We made another version of Chris Clown's Crazy Car which did this, but felt that

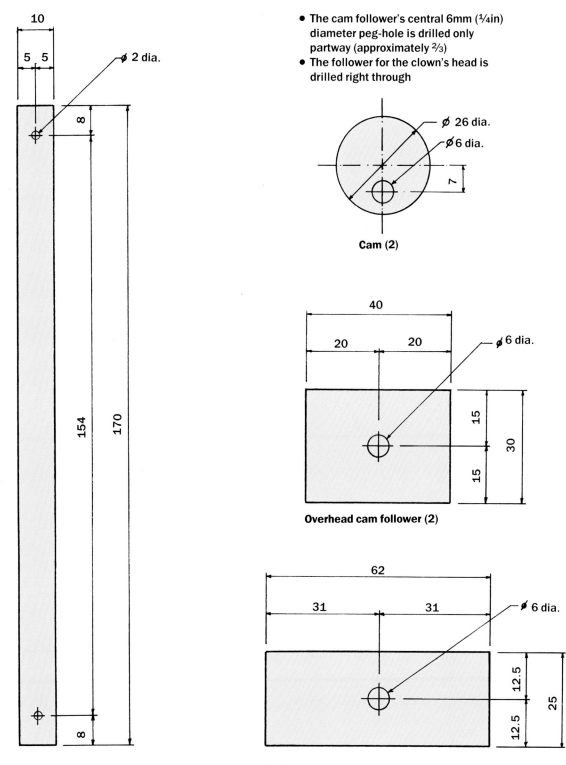

- The cam follower's central 6mm (¼in) diameter peg-hole is drilled only partway (approximately ⅔)
- The follower for the clown's head is drilled right through

ø 26 dia.

ø 6 dia.

**Cam (2)**

ø 2 dia.

**Follower connecting strip (2)**

ø 6 dia.

**Overhead cam follower (2)**

ø 6 dia.

**Follower connected to clown's head**

*Fig 9.4*
**Cams, followers and connecting strips.**

it detracted from the actions of Chris's head, the bonnet and the boot.

### Chris Clown's head

Chris Clown's head is made from a 32mm (1¼in) diameter wooden bead. His nose is also a wooden bead that is attached with a 3mm (⅛in) dowel peg. The size of Chris's nose is entirely up to you (although, as previously explained, a large nose is prone to hitting the windscreen). We suggest a bead diameter size between 6mm (¼in) and 10mm (⅜in).

Make sure that you hold the nose and head securely in a vice when drilling the small peg holes in each. If you have one, use a hand drill – it will give you much better control.

Drill a hole in the base of Chris's head to take the 6mm (¼in) dowel (his neck) which is attached to the follower.

Paint Chris's head.

### Final assembly

With the painting complete, fix the bonnet and boot lids to the car using 16mm (⅝in) brass hinges and small screws. Refer to Fig 9.1 for a guide to assembling the toy.

Hold the car upside down and place Chris's head follower into position. Place the cam followers into position so their connection strips are resting on the follower of Chris's head. Next, pass an axle rod through the axle hole on one of the sides, slide a cam onto it and pass the axle rod through the other side. Do the same with the other axle rod and cam. Now dry assemble the wheels to the axle rods. Fig 9.5 shows the cam system in place.

Turn each set of wheels until the cams both have their follower pegs to their lowest possible position. With a sharp pencil, mark the position of the top of the car onto the follower pegs. Dismantle the car and cut the follower pegs to size at the pencil mark. Reassemble the car, this time gluing the cams to the centre of the axle rods.

If you want the bonnet to open at the same moment as the boot, make sure that the cams are in exactly the same position as each other. However, if you wish them to alternate in opening and closing, simply turn one set of wheels only until they are in opposite positions (see **Fig 9.1**).

Glue the wheels and then Chris's head onto his neck.

Attach the cord to the car's mouth and Chris is ready to go!

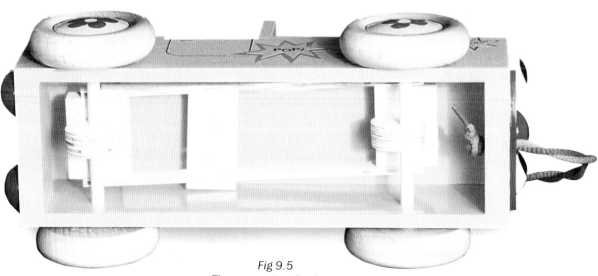

*Fig 9.5*
**The cam system in place.**

*Fig 9.6*
**The bonnet and boot can open at the same time —
or alternately (bottom).**

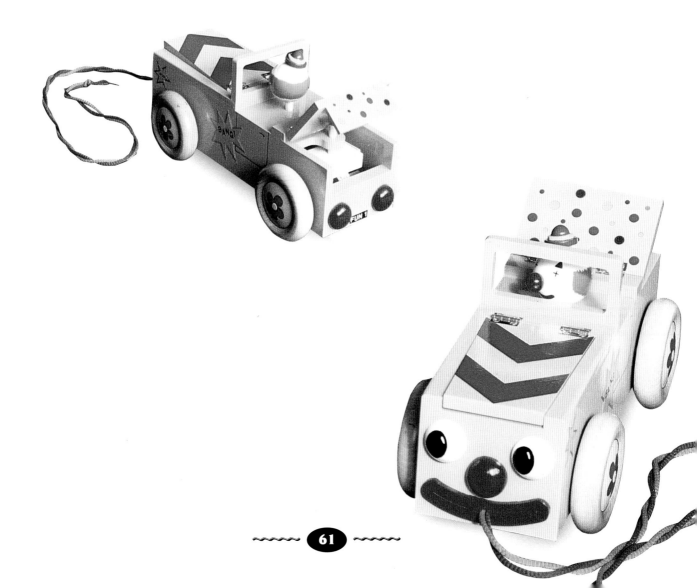

# Flying Kite

**N**o need to worry if the weather is bad outside, a child may fly this kite in his bedroom!

By alternately tugging gently on each bead, the kite will ascend towards the sun and clouds. Slacken the tension on the strings and the kite will come back down to earth.

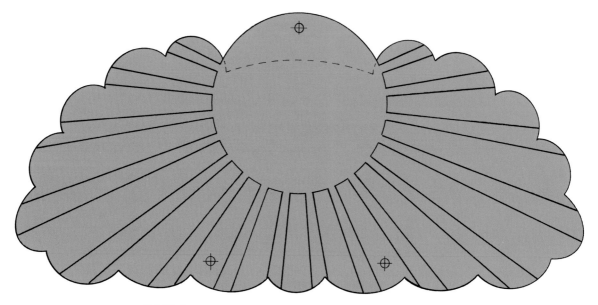

Fig 10.1

**The sun and cloud are both cut from 3mm (⅛in) ply.**

All holes 3mm (⅛in) dia.

**CUTTING LIST**

| | | |
|---|---|---|
| (All birch plywood) | | **Miscellaneous** |
| Kite: | 120 x 80 x 12mm | (2) beads |
| | (4¾ x 3³/₁₆ x ½in) | String |
| Sun: | 200 x 95 x 3mm | Fabric/plastic tail for kite |
| | (8 x 3¾ x ⅛in) | |
| Cloud: | 200 x 90 x 3mm | |
| | (8 x 3⁹/₁₆ x ⅛in) | |

## Construction

### Sun and clouds

Prepare a suitably sized piece of 3mm (⅛in) birch plywood. Transfer the cloud and sun profiles onto it (see **Fig 10.1**). Remember that the sun is cut out separately from the cloud – they are fixed together later on.

**Tip** Mark and cut the sun's rays a little longer than necessary. This will aid the cleaning up of the edge of the cloud at a later stage.

Drill all the holes marked. We used a 2.5mm (³/₃₂in) diameter drill bit, but the size required will vary dependent upon the thickness of string you plan to use. Ensure that the string passes freely through the holes.

Fretsaw out the profiles.

Glue the sun and its rays onto the cloud. Pin each ray to the cloud to aid adhesion. Use 18mm (¾in) pins and try not to drive them right through the cloud. When the glue has set, the protruding pins may be carefully removed using pincers. Fill the pin holes with wood filler.

With the sun and cloud facing downwards carefully fretsaw off the surplus length of the sun's rays using the edge of the clouds as a guide.

### Kite

Prepare a piece of 12mm (½in) plywood. Transfer the kite profile onto it and cut it out (see **Fig 10.2**).

Prior to drilling the two string holes (see dotted detail lines on **Fig 10.2**), mark the entry and exit points of each hole. From each of the kite's side points, mark 15mm (⅝in) along the top edge and 12mm (½in) along the bottom edge. Using a square, mark a line across each edge from these points and find the centre of this line.

It is useful to draw a line from the position of the top of the holes to the position of the bottom of the holes on the front face side of the kite. These lines will aid you when drilling the string holes.

Hold the kite in a bench vice, ensuring that the hole to be drilled is in a vertical position. Using a hand drill and bit, drill out each hole in turn. The diameter of these holes are dependent upon the thickness of string you plan to use. The string must pass freely through the holes, but not too loosely!

Cut two equal lengths of string for the kite strings – the length is dependent upon the overall height you wish the kite to fly. Thread each length of string through the side holes of the kite and then through the holes in the cloud. Knot each one behind the cloud so they cannot be pulled back through. Thread a bead to the bottom end of each string and tie knots so the beads are securely retained.

You may find that the hole in each bead needs enlarging in order to allow the string to pass through. If so, ensure that each bead is held securely in a vice while drilling.

Knot the end of a short length of string and pass the unknotted end through the hole in the sun. This string is for hanging up the toy.

*Fig 10.2*
**The kite. See text for hole diameters and positioning.**

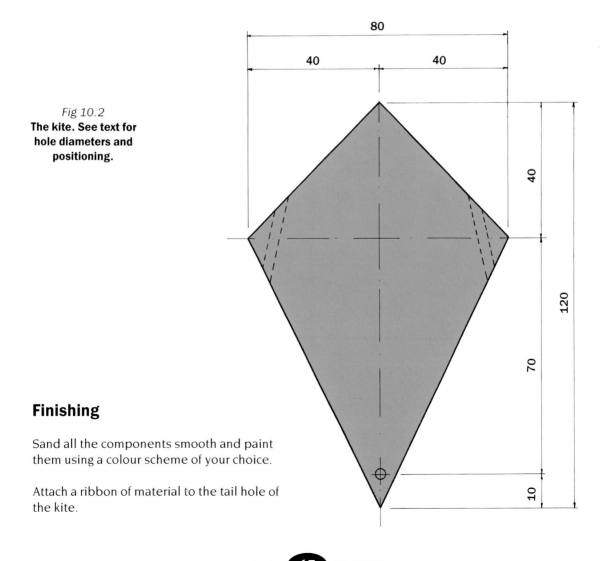

## Finishing

Sand all the components smooth and paint them using a colour scheme of your choice.

Attach a ribbon of material to the tail hole of the kite.

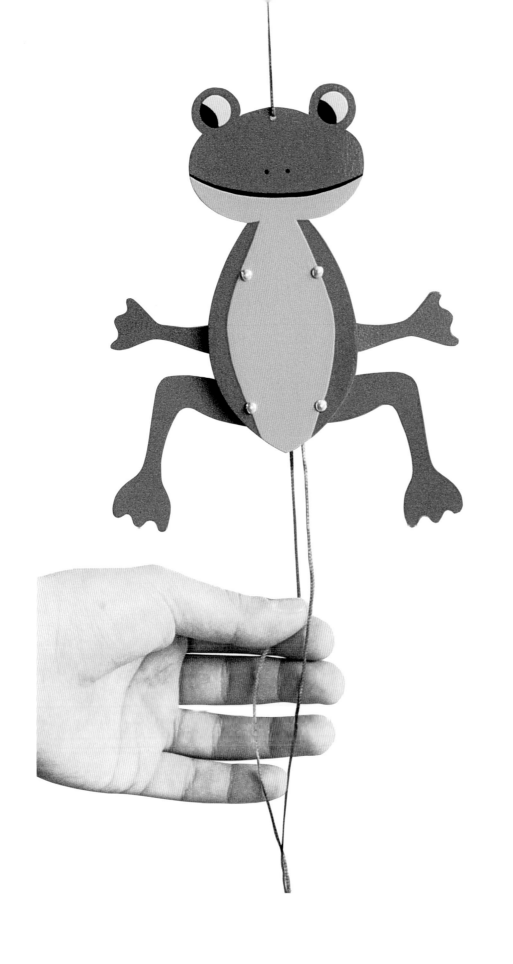

ELEVEN

# Freda the Frog

Freda the Frog is a fun toy that has proved to be very popular with Luke, our son, and his friends.

She may be hung from a door, shelf or wall. A gentle tug on her cord pull will make her arms and/or legs rise up and down. Repetitive tugs make Freda appear to be swimming.

Freda is an excellent toy for the younger child. Toddlers love to copy her actions and sing along when she is operated in conjunction with her own special song (sung to the popular tune of 'The Wheels Of The Bus Go Round And Round').

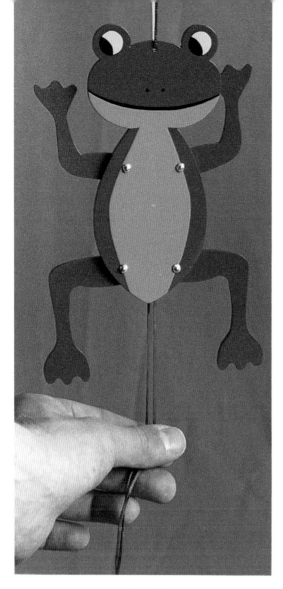

Fig 11.1
**Operating the legs and arms together.**

## Freda's song

1 Fre – da the frog swims round the pond,
          round the pond,
          round the pond.
Freda the frog swims round the pond, all day long.

2 Freda the Frog flaps her arms,
          flaps her arms,
          flaps her arms,
  Freda the Frog flaps her arms, all day long.

3 Freda the Frog kicks her legs,
          kicks her legs,
          kicks her legs,
  Freda the Frog kicks her legs, all day long.

**CUTTING LIST**

Scraps of 3mm (⅛in) birch plywood
(4) 2.4mm diameter rivets
Cord
(8) washers

## Construction

Transfer the full-size outlines of Freda's body, arms and legs onto 3mm (⅛in) birch plywood and cut out using a fretsaw (see **Fig 11.3**).

Drill the rivet holes. 2.4mm diameter rivets were used on the toy shown, so 3mm (⅛in) holes were drilled.

The smaller holes, next to the rivet holes, on the arms and legs should be drilled with a 2mm (³⁄₃₂in) drill bit.

A 2mm (³⁄₃₂in) hole is also drilled at the centre top of Freda's head. Her hanging cord is attached to this when construction is complete.

Freda is now ready to be painted prior to assembly.

## Assembly

When the painting is complete, loosely rivet the arms and legs to Freda's body. Washers can be inserted between arms, legs and body to ensure free movement of her limbs.

**Tip** It is easier to pass the arm-and-leg joining threads through the appropriate small holes before riveting. This will save your time and patience as it can prove awkward to thread the arms and legs after riveting (see **Fig 11.4**).

Finally, attach the pull cord and hanging cord as shown in the photograph.

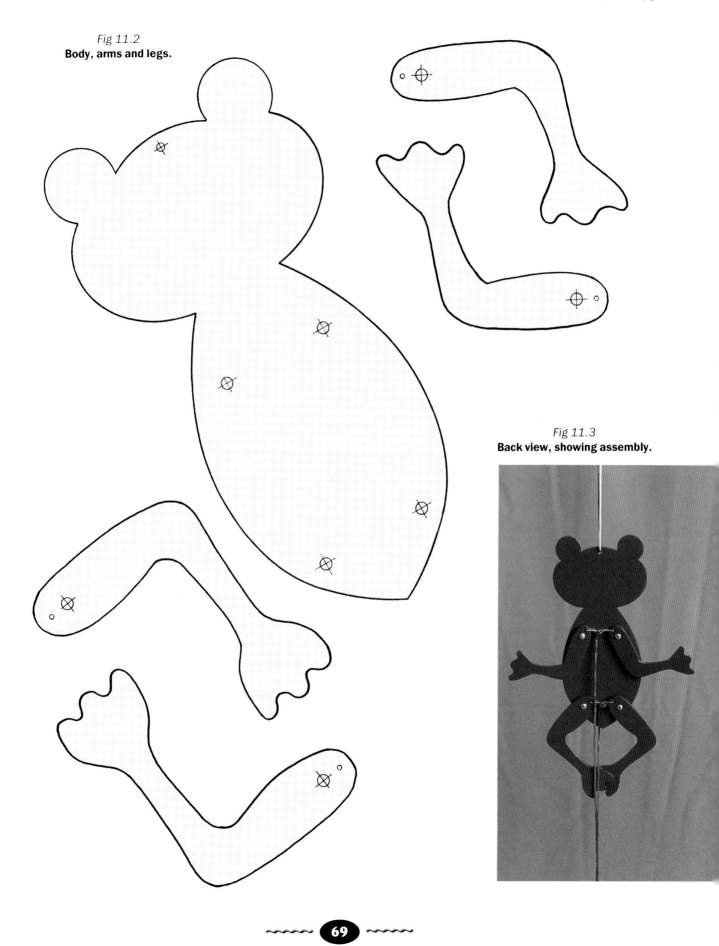

*Fig 11.2*
**Body, arms and legs.**

*Fig 11.3*
**Back view, showing assembly.**

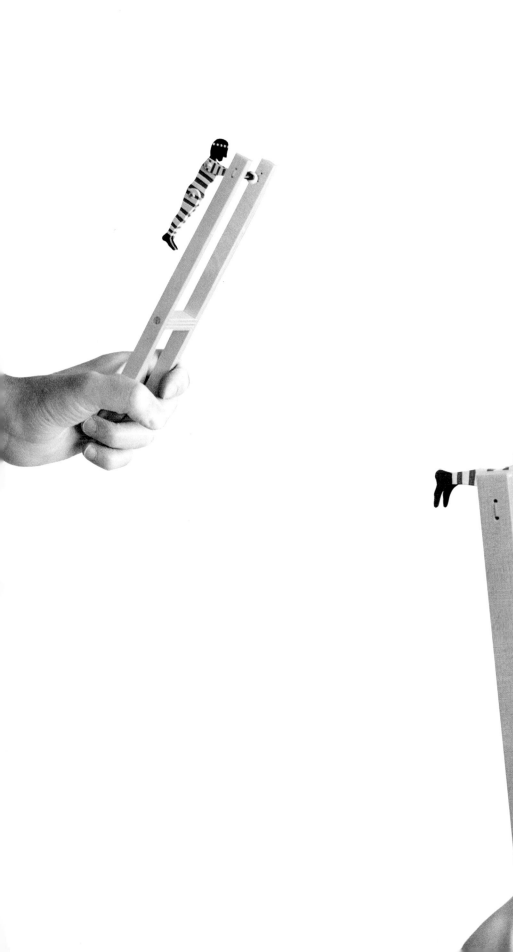

# Gymnast

You may be familiar with this traditional acrobatic toy, but we offer no excuses for including it in this book as its appeal to children never seems to diminish.

The design shown may be a little smaller than ones that you have come across before. This is because, in the past, we have made larger versions, and some children with small hands found them difficult to operate. Of course, you may enlarge the size of the design if required.

The gymnast is operated by holding her upright and gently squeezing and releasing the base of the frame. In this way the gymnast can perform a variety of somersaults and tricks!

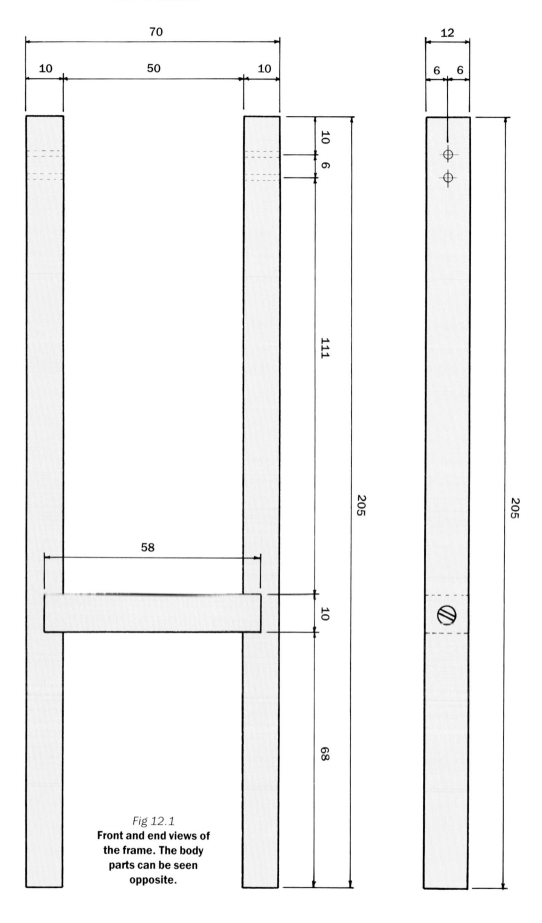

Fig 12.1
**Front and end views of
the frame. The body
parts can be seen
opposite.**

---

### CUTTING LIST

| | | |
|---|---|---|
| (All birch plywood) | | **Miscellaneous** |
| Upright (2): | 205 x 12 x 10mm<br>(8¹/₁₆ x ½ x ³/₈in) | A small bead 10mm (³/₈in) diameter or smaller |
| Crosspiece: | 58 x 12 x 10mm<br>(2⁹/₃₂ x ½ x ³/₈in) | (2) 18mm (¾in) No. 4 brass countersunk<br>screws |
| Gymnast: | scrap piece of 3mm<br>(¹/₈in) plywood | (4) rivets 2.44mm diameter |

---

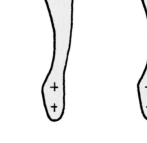

All body parts are from 3mm (¹/₈in) thick birch plywood

## Construction

### Gymnast

The body, legs and arms of the gymnast are all cut from 3mm (¹/₈in) thick birch plywood using a fretsaw (see **Fig 12.1**). It is easier to drill all the holes prior to cutting out. The hole diameters will be determined by the size of rivets that you choose to use.

Paint the gymnast before assembling her.

### Frame

Each of the frame upright sides have two holes drilled at the top, the diameter of which will be dependent on the thickness of the gymnast supporting cord you use. We suggest that they should be approximately 1–2mm (approximately ¹/₁₆in) in diameter.

A slot of the same thickness as the plywood (10mm (³/₈in)) is cut halfway into the thickness of each of the frame uprights. These are to accommodate the horizontal crosspiece which joins the uprights together.

To cut these slots, first mark a halfway dividing line along the side of the uprights (a correctly set marking gauge is ideal for this purpose). Using a set square, draw lines across the inside face of the uprights and down the sides until they meet the previously marked halfway dividing line. These lines indicate where to make the saw cuts. Make absolutely sure that the marked slots are exactly the right size to accommodate the crosspiece before cutting out.

Use a fine-toothed saw to cut down the inside side of the slot lines (see **Fig 12.2(a)**). It is wise to make an extra saw cut down the central waste piece of the slots (see **Fig 12.2(b)**). This will make the next stage, chiselling out the waste, much easier.

Using a chisel, pare away the waste (see **Fig 12.2(c)**). It is best to remove the waste pieces a little at a time, as you could damage the uprights by trying to remove them in one go.

The crosspiece should fit snugly into the uprights. A sloppy fit is obviously no good, and too tight a fit may cause the uprights to split

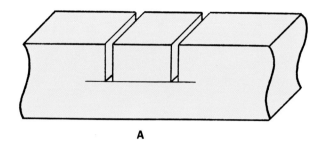

A

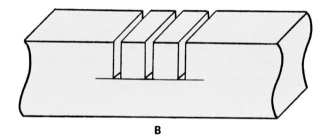

B

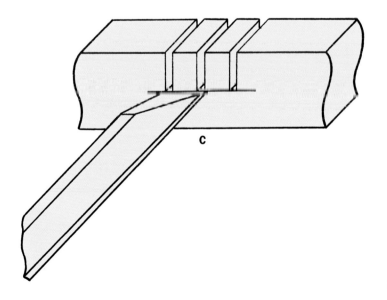

C

Fig 12.2
**Cutting out the slots on the frame.**

when the toy is in use.

Finely sand the frame uprights and crosspiece and assemble with glue.

It is advisable to lightly clamp the assembled frame until the glue sets – overnight in a vice is sufficient. For extra strength an 18mm (¾in) No. 4 brass screw may be inserted through the side of each upright and into the crosspiece as illustrated in Fig 12.1.

## Final assembly

Figure 12.3 shows a frontal view of the final positioning of the cord in relation to the gymnast, bead and frame. Use this as a guide to assembly.

Make sure that you knot the cord at the side of one of the uprights. Dab a little glue onto the knot and allow to dry before operating the toy. This glue should stop the knot from working loose.

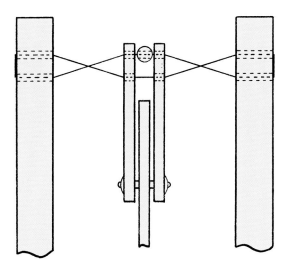

*Fig 12.3*
**Partial front view of the gymnast and frame, illustrating cord arrangement.**

# THIRTEEN

# Hang-on-Hank & Bucking Billy

Cowhand Hank rides the most stubborn horse on the ranch – Bucking Billy. Billy bucks and kicks and does all he can to annoy Hank!

Every morning Hank saddles up Billy and rides out to check the cattle. As he rides out, all the ranch hands call out, 'HANG ON, HANK!'.

This is a pull-along toy. Billy, the horse, is fitted to a base which has four wheels. The two back wheels are larger than the front ones and are offset, enabling Billy to kick and buck.

Hank has a peg fitted to the inside of his right hand. This fits into a hole on Billy's neck, thus helping Hank to hang on.

Hank's limbs are loosely riveted to allow free movement when riding Billy. By riveting Hank's joints together more firmly, he can be posed more easily for play both off and on his horse.

The degree of Billy's buck depends upon how far offset you drill the axle holes in the rear wheels. If you do not wish Billy to buck at all, simply fit equal-sized wheels all round and do not offset the axles.

Rodeo games may be played with Hank and Billy. Place Hank in the saddle without fitting his peg into Billy's neck. Then quickly pull Billy along and see how long Hank can hang on!

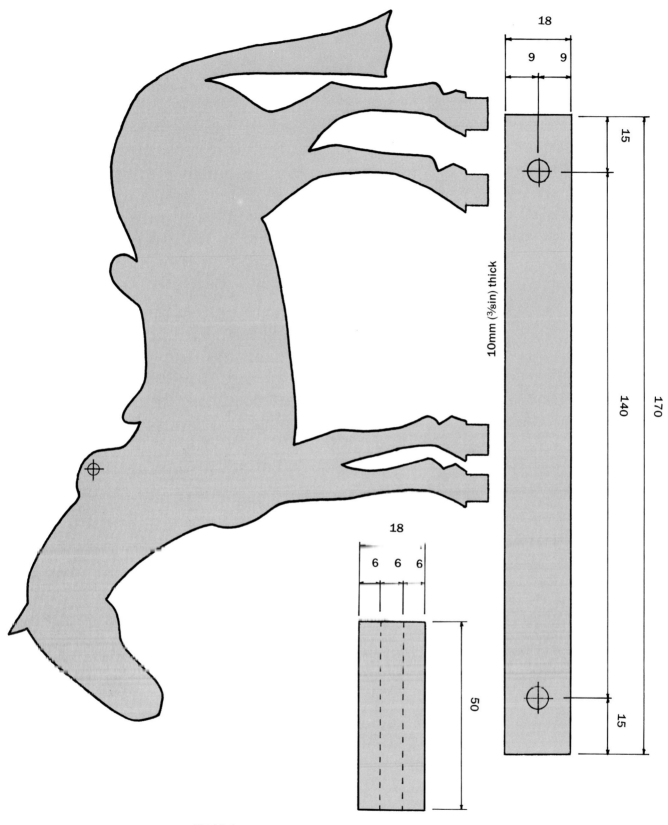

18

9    9

15

10mm (³⁄₈in) thick

140    170

18

6   6   6

50

15

Fig 13.1
**Horse (Bucking Billy) and base (front and side
view).**

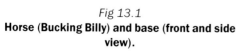

## CUTTING LIST

*(All birch plywood)*
Hank: small quantity of 10mm *(3/8in)* and
   3mm *(1/8in)*
Bucking Billy: 200 x 140 x 10mm *(8 x 5 1/2 x*
   *3/8in)*
Base: 170 x 50 x 18mm *(6 11/16 x 2 x 3/4in)*

**Miscellaneous**
(2) 38mm *(1 1/2in)* diameter wood wheels
(2) 63mm *(2 1/2in)* diameter wood wheels
Length of 6mm *(1/4in)* dowel rod
(4) washers to fit 6mm *(1/4in)* dowel rod
(4) snap rivets
Small piece of 3mm *(1/8in)* dowel rod
Screw eyelet
Length of string/cord

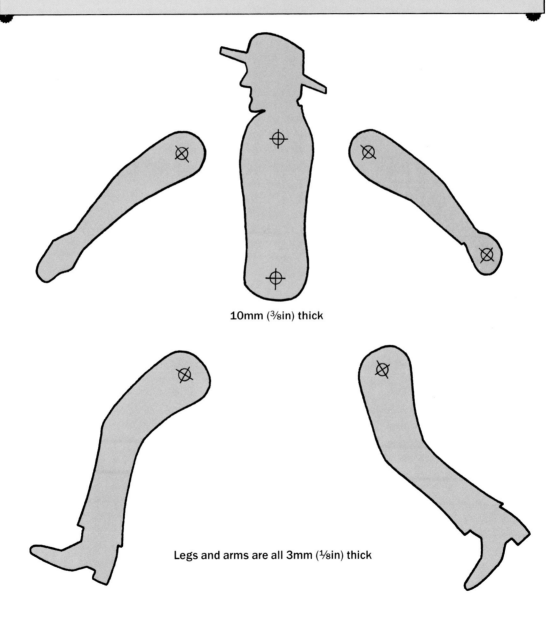

10mm *(3/8in)* thick

Legs and arms are all 3mm *(1/8in)* thick

*Fig 13.2*
**The combined head and torso, legs and arms.**

*Fig 13.3*
**Hank holds tight . . .**

*Fig 13.4*
**. . . Billy starts to
dislodge him . . .**

## Construction

### Bucking Billy

Transfer the outline of Billy, the horse, onto
10mm (⅜in) birch plywood and cut out
(see **Fig 13.1**).

Drill the peg hole in Billy's neck which will
later enable Hank to 'hold the reins'. We
used a 3mm (⅛in) dowel for Hank's peg, so
we drilled the peg hole with a 3.5mm (⁵⁄₃₂in)
drill bit. This allowed Hank's peg, especially
after painting, to fit in and be taken out
easily.

Cut Billy's base from either plywood or a
suitable hardwood such as beech.

Drill the holes for the 6mm (¼in) diameter
dowel axle rods. Use a drill bit which will
enable the axles to turn freely.

Draw a central line lengthways on the top
surface of the base. Stand Billy centrally on
this line and mark the positions of his
attaching lugs (the tenons that extend from the
base of his hooves).

Using a suitably sized chisel – 3 or 6mm (⅛ or
¼in) – carefully chop out the waste to create
slots (mortices) to receive the lugs (tenons).

**Tip** The bulk of the waste can be removed
by drilling a hole, or holes, to the correct
depth first.

Using glue, fix Billy to his base. He may now
be painted.

Sand a length of 6mm (¼in) dowel rod and cut
out the front and rear axle rods. 38mm (1½in)
ready-made wood wheels are used at the front
and 63mm (2½in) at the rear. The rear wheel
axle is offset by 16mm (⅝in). Plug the original
hole with dowel (or wood filler, if necessary)
before drilling the offset hole. We suggest that
this is the absolute maximum for 63mm (2½in)
diameter wheels.

If required, paint or varnish the wheels before
assembly. Remember to fit washers between
the wheels and the base.

Centrally fit an eyelet to the front of Billy's
base. Attach a length of cord, and Billy is ready
to go!

Fig 13.5

**. . . Hank is in trouble . . .**

## Hang-on-Hank

Transfer the outline of Hank's head and torso to 10mm (³⁄₈in) birch plywood and his arms and legs to 3mm (¹⁄₈in) birch plywood (see **Fig 13.2**). Prior to cutting these out it is advisable to drill the holes for the rivets. The diameters will depend upon the size of rivets that you wish to use.

Cut a 10mm (³⁄₈in) length of 3mm (¹⁄₈in) dowel. Drill a hole in Hank's right hand to provide a snug fit for this dowel. Then glue the dowel into place.

Paint Hank's body parts before assembly (*see* 'Riveting' in Construction Techniques chapter pages 13–15).

*Fig 13.6*

**. . . Hank falls off!**

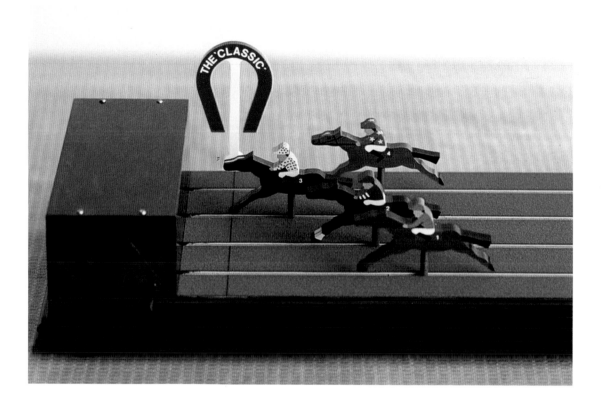

FOURTEEN

# Classic Racing

**B**ring the excitement of flat racing to your home table top!

In this thrilling game, players own horses and run them in races, including the Classic.

Each horse is connected to an undertrack slideway. A cord is attached to the base of each horse, runs up each slideway and is fixed to a winch inside the end box. When the handle of the winch is turned the horses 'run' along the track. As the cords wrap around the winch they will inevitably wind up at different rates. This ensures a random winner for every race!

The inspiration for this game came from a similar one that Jeff made for his family to play during Christmas 1984. The track looked similar, except that rails were fitted to the sides. The horses and their jockeys, however, were entirely different – in the original game they were converted from American Civil War cavalry toy soldiers!

## CUTTING LIST

| | | | |
|---|---|---|---|
| Track base: | 860 x 194 x 18mm<br>(33⅞ x 7⅝ x ¾in)<br>MDF | Winch box glue block: | 170 x 9mm<br>(6¹¹⁄₁₆ x ⅜in)<br>quadrant |
| Slideway slats (5): | 854 x 22 x 12mm<br>(33⅝ x ⅞ x ½in)<br>plywood | Winch: | 204 x 18mm<br>(8¹⁄₃₂ x ¾in) diameter<br>ramin dowel |
| Track turf slats (3): | 788 x 37 x 3mm<br>(31 x 1⁷⁄₁₆ x ⅛in)<br>plywood | | |
| Track turf slats (2): | 788 x 29.5 x 3mm<br>(31¹⁄₃₂ x 1⁵⁄₃₂ x ⅛in)<br>plywood | **Miscellaneous**<br>(1) 25mm (*1in*) wood wheel<br>Scraps of 6mm (*¼in*) plywood for handle<br>Scraps of 10mm (*⅜in*) plywood for horses | |
| Winch box front: | 194 x 53 x 6mm<br>(7⅝ x 2³⁄₃₂ x ¼in)<br>plywood |   and their bases<br>Length of 6mm (*¼in*) dowel<br>(4) screw eyelets | |
| Winch box back: | 194 x 62 x 6mm<br>(7⅝ x 2⁷⁄₁₆ x ¼in)<br>plywood | Cord<br>(4) rubber 'buffers'<br>Moulding strip to edge the track (optional) | |
| Winch box sides (2): | 60 x 50 x 12mm<br>(2⅜ x 2 x ½in)<br>plywood | 788 x 194mm (31¹⁄₃₂ x 7⅝in) green velour<br>  for turf<br>(2) 18mm (¾in) No. 4 countersunk screws | |
| Winch box top: | 194 x 72 x 3mm<br>(7⅝ x 2¹³⁄₁₆ x ⅛in)<br>plywood | (4) 10mm (⅜in) No. 2 roundhead screws | |

## Construction

### The horses and jockeys

These are fretsawed out of 10mm (⅜in) birch plywood. Each is then placed squarely, upside down, into a vice and a 4.5mm (³⁄₁₆in) diameter hole is drilled 6mm (¼in) deep into the horse's belly (see **Fig 14.1**).

The stands for the horses (which will slide along underneath the track's surface) are cut from 10mm (⅜in) birch plywood (see **Fig 14.2**). A 4.5mm (³⁄₁₆in) diameter hole is drilled, centrally, right the way through it.

Each horse's connecting rod is 40mm (1⁹⁄₁₆in) long and is cut from a length of 4.5mm (1⁹⁄₁₆in) diameter ramin dowel.

Glue one end of the connecting rod into the belly hole of the horse and glue the other into the hole in the stand. When the glue has set, sand any protrusions from the underside of the stand.

Screw a small screw eyelet to the front centre of each stand.

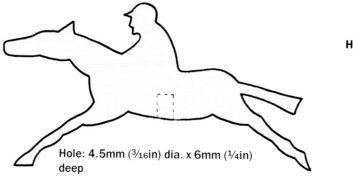

*Fig 14.1*
**Horse and jockey.**

Hole: 4.5mm (³⁄₁₆in) dia. x 6mm (¼in) deep

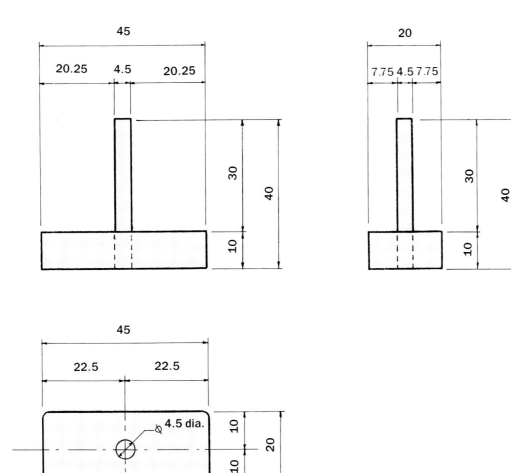

Corners have 1.5mm radii

*Fig 14.2*
**Horse and jockey stand and connecting rod.**

## The track

Glue and pin the 12mm (½in) birch plywood slideway slats to the 18mm (¾in) MDF base (see **Figs 14.3 and 14.4**). MDF was chosen for its relative stability, but plywood or chipboard could be used. Ensure that the slats are pinned flush to one end (the start end), so as to allow a 6mm (¼in) space at the other end (necessary for fitting the winch box). Fig 14.5 shows the slats secured to the MDF base, and also shows clearly how the back of the winch box fits into the 6mm (¼in) space.

## The winch box

The winch box is made up separately from the track. You will see in Fig 14.6 that it is a straightforward box construction. The front and back pieces are simply glued and pinned to the sides. However, before doing this, drill the 18mm (¾in) hole in each side piece. This hole will allow the winch (18mm [¾in] dowel) to turn freely in each end.

Do not glue and pin the top of the box on, this will be held in place later with screws.

Glue a length of 9mm (⅜in) quadrant to the bottom of the inside front edge of the winch box. When the glue has set, glue the winch box into position on the track (see **Fig 14.5**). Drive a few moulding pins through the bottom of the back piece into the slideway slats.

Fig 14.3
**End view of track highlighting the slideways.**

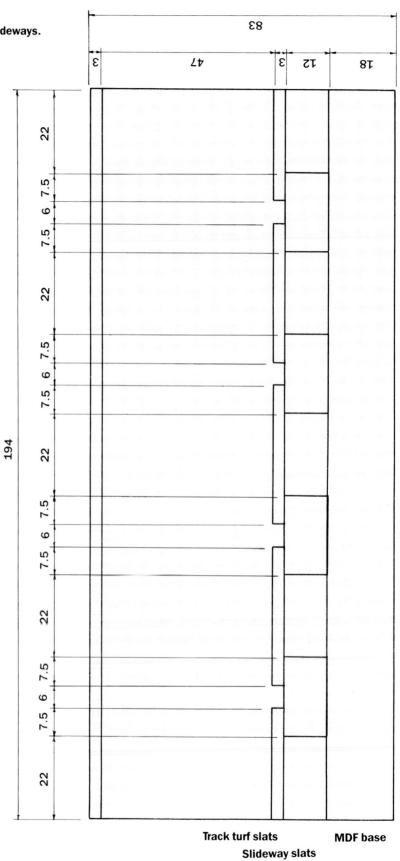

**Track turf slats**

**Slideway slats**

**MDF base**

**Moulded edging, winch and winning
post removed for clarity**

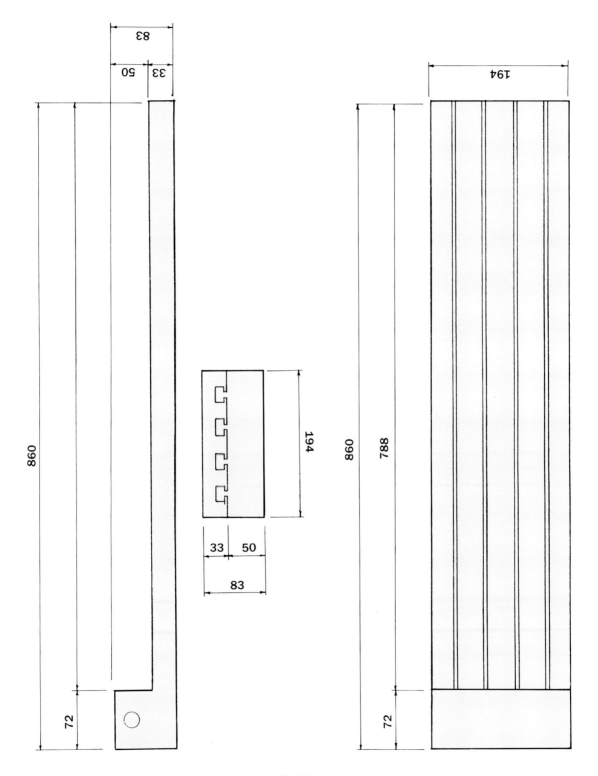

*Fig 14.4*
**The track (side, plan and end views).**

## The winch and handle

The winch is cut from 18mm (¾in) ramin dowel. Hold the dowel in a vice or other suitable clamping system and drill the four 2mm (³⁄₃₂in) cord-fixing holes into it (see **Fig 14.7**).

The handle is cut from 6mm (¼in) birch plywood. It is advisable to drill the holes into it (for the winch and handle rod) before cutting out. Cut the handle rod from 6mm (¼in) ramin dowel and glue into position. The handle may now be glued to one end of the winch (see **Fig 14.8**). At the other end a ready-made 25mm (1in) diameter wood wheel is screwed on (see **Fig 14.9**). Use a brass 18mm (¾in) No. 4 countersunk screw. The wheel is screwed on rather than glued so that the wheel can be easily removed to allow the winch to be removable if required.

We used four 10mm (³⁄₈in) No. 2 roundhead screws to hold the box top in place. Two are situated at each side, driven into the boxed sides (see **Fig 14.8**). Ensure that they are either side of the winch hole. This will enable the top to be removed to gain access to the winch for fixing or adjusting the cords.

Glue and pin the 3mm (⅛in) track 'turf' slats onto the slideway slats (see **Fig 14.4**). If cut out and fitted correctly the horses should slide freely up the track. Place the horses into position and test this by manually sliding each horse up the track.

If a horse tends to stick at a certain point either shave a little off the sides of the horse's stands or, using a 3mm (⅛in) thick sanding stick (see **page 3**), sand a little from the offending edges of the 'turf' slats.

You may wish to cover the MDF edges with a strip of moulding. Be careful not to cover over the entrances to the slideways, otherwise the fitting or removal of the horses will not be possible!

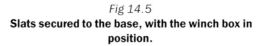

*Fig 14.5*
**Slats secured to the base, with the winch box in position.**

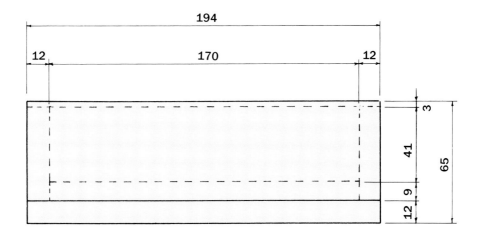

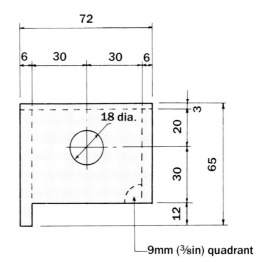

18 dia.

9mm (³⁄₈in) quadrant

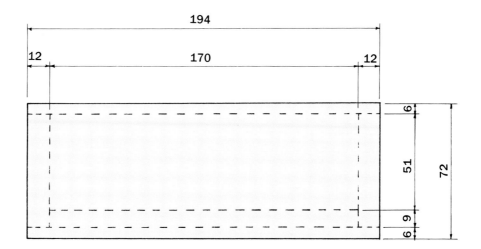

*Fig 14.6*
**Front, end and plan views of the winch box.**

*Fig 14.7*
**Winch and handle (end, front and plan views).**

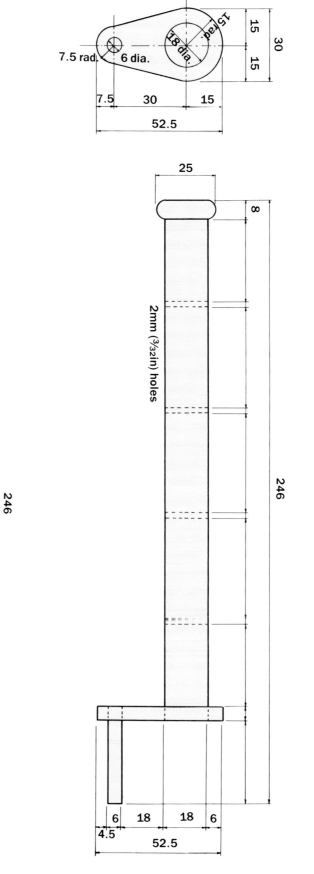
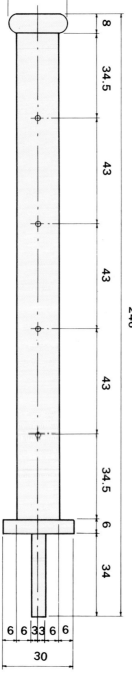

*Fig 14.8*
**The handle glued to the winch, and the box top
screwed in place.**

*Fig 14.9*
**The wood wheel and winning post screwed in
position.**

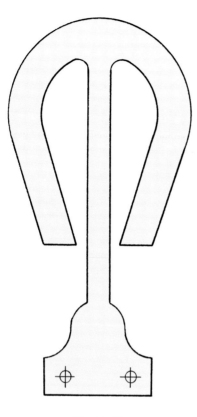

*Fig 14.10*
**The winning post.**

## Winning post

The winning post is fretsawed from 6mm (¼in) birch plywood (see **Fig 14.10**). Ours is screwed to the side of the track at the finishing line using two 18mm (¾in) No. 4 brass screws (see **Fig 14.9**).

For easier removal of the winning post (for storage purposes), two 3mm (⅛in) pegs could be used instead of screws. Cut these pegs from a length of 3mm (⅛in) ramin dowel. You will notice that in Fig 14.10 the diameter of the holes has not been given. The size will depend upon which option you choose.

## Horse-return paddle

The horse-return paddle is cut from 6mm (¼in) birch plywood (see **Fig 14.11**). A piece of sticky-backed plastic is used to cover the bottom edge. This will help protect the velour 'turf' when pulling the horses back to their starting positions.

*Fig 14.11*
**The horse-return paddle.**

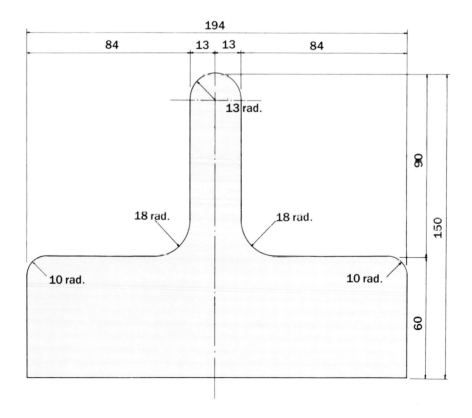

## Finishing

### Track

Before 'laying the turf', apply a finish to the track. Paint, stain and/or varnish to a style of your own choosing.

Remove the winch handle and the winch box lid and finish them separately. We finished ours by first staining it with a Victorian mahogany spirit stain. This coloured the ramin moulding beautifully, but, unfortunately, the plywood was a shade too pink for our taste (our fault for not testing on a scrap piece first!). To remedy this we varnished the track with a deep red mahogany stained varnish.

Fit rubber buffers to the underside of the track to protect the surface of the table used for play.

### Horses and jockeys

When painting the jockey's 'silks' feel free to make up your own patterns and colour schemes. Each horse should have a number (1–4).

### Finishing post

Paint and decorate to your own requirements before attaching to the track. (Attach after laying the turf.)

### Laying the 'turf'

Cut a piece of green self-adhesive velour slightly larger than the width and length of the track to be covered. Starting at one end, peel a little of the velour's backing sheet away and stick the velour down flush with the front side of the winch box. Do not worry that you are covering over the gaps between the slats, these will be trimmed later.

Slowly peel the rest of the backing sheet away, while evenly pressing down the rest of the velour. When you have laid the velour, finish pressing it down using a COLD iron. Pay particular attention to the edges and ensure that there are no air bubbles. Use a very sharp knife (preferably a modelling knife or scalpel)

to trim the velour from the edges. At the top of each of the slat's gap, pierce through the velour with the knife. Then slowly pull the knife along each of the slat's edges. The surplus velour should trim easily away. If you find this difficult, then your knife blade is probably not sharp enough.

With the turf laid, you can mark the finishing and start line with a black ink Biro and a rule. The finish line is 30mm (1³⁄₁₆in) away from the front of the winch box (see **Fig 14.12**).

The start line is 100mm (4in) away from the other end.

## Stringing up the horses

Before stringing up the horses it is helpful to rub each horse stand with a candle. This aids the horses to run along the track smoothly.

For each horse cut a piece of strong, thin cord approximately 100mm (4in) longer than the track. Tie one end securely to the eyelet on the horse stand. Slide the horse onto the track and thread the cord along the slideway under the winch box. Thread the cord through the relevant cord hole (see **Fig 14.7**).

Repeat this for all the other horses.

Make absolutely sure that all the horses are equally alongside each other behind the start line. Either tie the cords to the winch or secure them using sticky tape.

The horses are now ready to race.

## Classic racing

### Equipment

- Classic Racing Game
- 4 Playing Cards: ace (representing 1), 2, 3, and 4
- 40 counters (tiddlywinks, buttons etc.)

### Object of the game

To be the player who amasses the most prize money (counters) at the end of six races.

Fig 14.12
**The finish line and finishing post.**

### Play *(for 4 players)*

Shuffle the cards and deal one to each player. The number on each player's card indicates which horse he will own for that particular race, i.e., if a player is dealt a two, he will own horse number two for the race.

The four horses are placed alongside each other behind the start line. The player who drew horse number one turns the handle to race the horses. The first horse to pass the winning post wins the race.

The turning of the winch handle is stopped and the following two horses are placed second and third.

Winnings
• The owner of the winning horse receives three counters.
• The owner of the second-place horse receives two counters.
• The owner of the third-placed horse receives one counter.

The horses are unwound and placed at the start again. The cards are reshuffled and dealt out to the players. Again the player who owns horse number one turns the winch handle. This process is carried out for five races, until the sixth and final race – the Classic!

### The Classic

The Classic race is run in the same way as the other races with the exception of the prize money.

Winnings
• The winner receives four counters.
• The second-place horse receives three counters.
• The third-place horse receives two counters.
• The fourth-place horse receives one counter.

After the Classic has been run the game is over. Each player totals up their prize money (counters). The player with the largest amount wins the game.

### Play *(for three players)*

Option A
The game is played in a similar manner to rules for four players except that, after the cards have been dealt, the surplus horse remains in the race but is not owned by any player.

If the unowned horse wins any prize money its winnings are removed from the game.

Fig 14.13
**The game ready to start.**

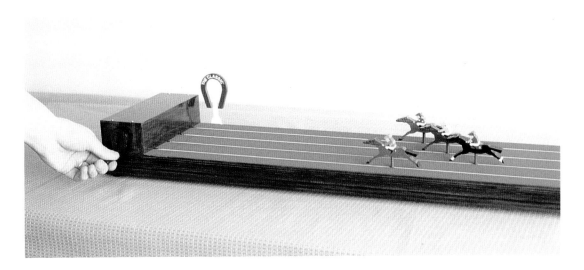

Option B
In this option the players take turns to own the
surplus horse in addition to their own.
Therefore, out of six races each player will own
two horses in two races.

To determine who will own this extra horse in
the Classic (and, therefore, have the
advantage, as the prize money is greater for
this race) the following must be undertaken at
the beginning of the game. Three of the
playing cards, one of which must be the ace,
are shuffled and dealt out. The player who
receives the ace will own the extra horse for
the Classic.

### Play *(for two players)*

In this variation each player will own and run
two horses in each race. When dealing out the
cards before each race, the players will receive
two cards each to determine the horses they
own.

### Winch operation

In order for the horses to successfully race,
resulting in a random winner, the winch handle
should be cranked as follows:
Four turns clockwise, two turns anticlockwise,
four turns clockwise, two turns anticlockwise
and so on until the end of the race.

We found this method the most exciting and
best suited for our track. Do experiment with
different cranking methods as your track may
suit a slightly different method.

*Fig 14.14*
**Turning the winch handle to race the horses.**

### Horse-return paddle

After each race the paddle is used to return
the horses equally behind the start line. To
operate, simply place the paddle in front of
the horses at the finish and, while turning the
winch handle anticlockwise, gently pull the
paddle backwards towards the start
(see **Fig 14.15**).

*Fig 14.15*
**Using the horse-return paddle to take the horses
back to the start.**

# FIFTEEN

# Horseshoe Hurling

**A** *participation theatre company that regularly toured Special Schools once asked Jeff to make this game for them. It was to be used in a tour with the theme 'The Wild West'.*

*During their adventure the children were invited to play the game. They loved it. The large horseshoes are easy to grip, and it is surprisingly simple to 'ring' the post.*

*The game may be played indoors or out. The base of the post is covered with a piece of carpet, which deadens the sound of the horseshoes ringing the post (a must for when the game is played early on Sunday morning!).*

*The game should only take an afternoon or so to construct, so, considering its play value (not forgetting its value in promoting eye-to-hand coordination) it makes an ideal project to make and give as a gift.*

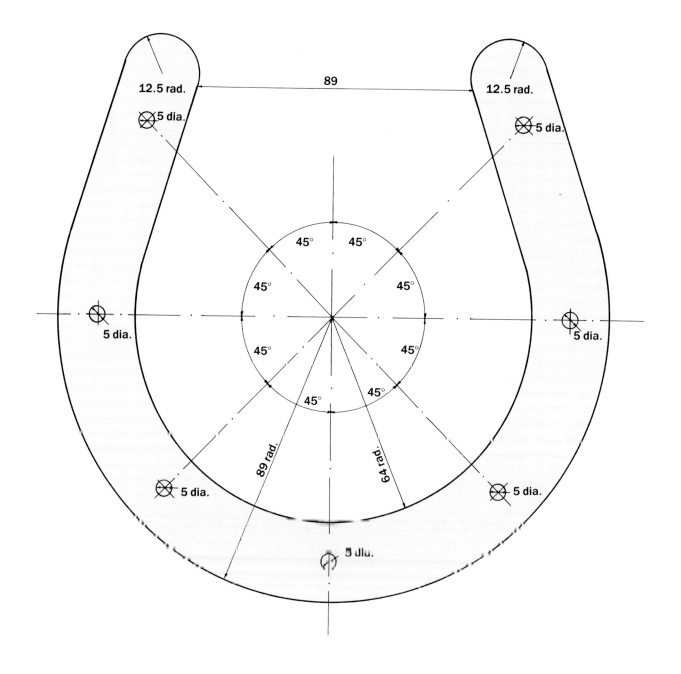

*Fig 15.1*
**Horseshoe.**

**CUTTING LIST**

| | |
|---|---|
| Post: | 400 x 25mm (15¾ x 1in) diameter ramin dowel |
| Base: | 310mm (12³⁄₁₆in) diameter circle of 12mm (½in) plywood |
| Horseshoe (4): | 178 x 178 x 10mm (7 x 7 x ⅜in) birch plywood |

**Miscellaneous**
310 x 310mm (12³⁄₁₆ x 12³⁄₁₆in) piece of carpet

## Construction

### Horseshoes

Use a fretsaw to cut out the four horseshoes (see **Fig 15.1**).

Drill the seven 'nail' holes in each one, using a 5mm (³⁄₁₆in) diameter drill bit.

### The post

Cut the post from a length of 25mm (1in) ramin dowel (see **Fig 15.2**). Slightly chamfer or round the top end.

Cut out the base of the post. If you wish, you could make it square instead of circular. If you do this, round off the corners.

Drill a 25mm (1in) diameter hole centrally in the base. We held our base securely in a bench vice (with a scrap piece of backing ply behind the hole area) and drilled the hole with an electric drill and a spade bit.

**Tip** Even though you may use a backing piece, it is a good idea that, when the central point of the spade bit just breaks through the base, you turn the base around the continue drilling from the other side. This should totally eradicate any 'split out' of the wood grain.

Glue the post into the hole in the base. When the glue has set, plane away any protrusion of the post on the underside.

To fit the carpet you must first cut out a 25mm (1in) diameter hole in the centre of your chosen piece. Then evenly spread plenty of Copydex glue onto the top surface of the base. Thread the carpet onto the post and press it firmly onto the base. When the glue has set, trim the surplus carpet away using a sharp knife.

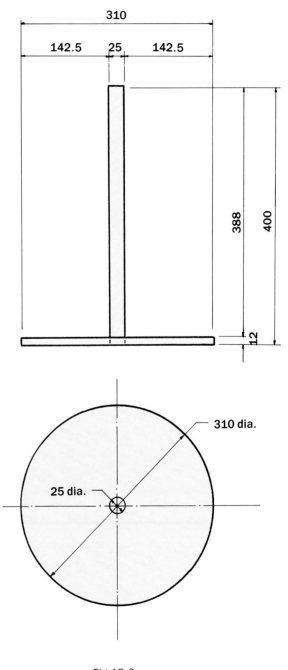

Fig 15.2
**The post and base.**

Fig 15.3
**Grip the horseshoe like this for maximum effectiveness.**

## Finishing

We left our horseshoe hurling set natural, applying no finishing at all. However, you could stain the horseshoes various colours. We do not recommend painting the horseshoes or the post as the paint will tend to chip off during use.

## Horseshoe hurling

### How to hurl the horseshoes

The way to hurl a horseshoe with maximum chance of it ringing the post is to hold it as shown in Fig 15.3. Then toss it, underarm, towards the post. In this way the horseshoe should spin through the air with the optimum opportunity for the open part of the shoe to ring the peg (if it is on target, of course!).

If it is held and thrown 'Frisbee' style (see **Fig 15.4**), the chances of the shoe ringing the post are greatly reduced. However this can add to the fun!

There are numerous ways in which this game can be played. No doubt you will have ideas of your own, but here is one way that is fun.

### Object of the game

To be the player who successfully rings the post with the horseshoes the most number of times.

Fig 15.4
**This technique reduces the chances of ringing the post, but can be great fun!**

## Play *(for two or more players)*

The players each take turns to throw the horseshoes.

A turn consists of four throws at the post.

A game consists of a predetermined number of turns (we suggest three or four to begin with).

Each individual player's turn takes place at progressively further distances from the post. For example, the first turn is taken 2 metres (2 yards) from the post. The second turn is taken 3 metres (3 yards) from the post. And so on.

Of course, if played indoors the size of your room will dictate the distances!

To successfully ring the post a horseshoe must end up around the post. It does not have to be touching it, but its inner area must contain the post. A horseshoe that rings the post but then spins away does not count.

Total a player's score after all four throws in a turn have been taken. Scoring horseshoes are only counted at the end of a turn as they can be knocked away by subsequent throws, in which case they do not count.

After each player has completed all of their turns, the one with the highest total of successfully ringed posts is the winner.

REPAIR DEPT

RECEPTION

Castrol
MOTOR OIL

SHOWROOM

DUNLOP

CHAMPION

Esso

SIXTEEN

# Loader's Garage

Loader's Garage has been designed as a versatile environment within which children can play with their own toy cars.

It differs from the more conventional toy garages in that the buildings are not attached to a baseboard. This is to allow children to design and change the layout of the garage complex themselves. Also, at the end of play, the buildings may be packed away easily into a drawer or toy cupboard.

Loader's Garage reflects a typical local garage. It is comprised of a large workshop; a car sales showroom; a shop for petrol sales and accessories; a car body repair shop with a spray booth; petrol pumps; a sign; and freestanding walls

All the buildings have removable roofs for increased play value.

## CUTTING LIST

**Body Repair Shop/Spray Booth**

| | |
|---|---|
| Side (2): | 280 x 50 x 6mm<br>(11 x 2 x ¼in) plywood |
| Front/Back/Middle (3): | 100 x 90 x 12mm<br>(4 x 3⁹/₁₆ x ½in)<br>plywood |
| Roof Section (2): | 284 x 78 x 3mm<br>(11⅛ x 3¹/₁₆ x ⅛in)<br>hardboard |
| Roof Locating Strips (4): | 50 x 9mm<br>(2 x ⅜in) quadrant |

**Workshop**

| | |
|---|---|
| Side (2): | 288 x 80 x 12mm<br>(11⁵/₁₆ x 3³/₃₂ x ½in)<br>plywood |
| Front/Back (2): | 248 x 120 x 6mm<br>(9¾ x 4¾ x ¼in)<br>plywood |
| Roof Section: | 304 x 132 x 3mm<br>(12 x 5³/₁₆ x ⅛in)<br>hardboard |
| Roof Section: | 304 x 140 x 3mm<br>(12 x 5½ x ⅛in)<br>hardboard |
| Roof Locating Strips (4): | 110 x 9mm<br>(4⁵/₁₆ x ⅜in) quadrant |

**Car Showroom and Shop**

| | |
|---|---|
| Side/Middle Wall (3): | 138 x 100 x 12mm<br>(5⁷/₁₆ x 4 x ½in)<br>plywood |
| Front/Back (2): | 300 x 73 x 6mm<br>(11¹³/₁₆ x 2⅞ x ¼in)<br>plywood |
| Roof Section: | 304 x 90 x 3mm<br>(12 x 3¹⁷/₃₂ x ⅛in)<br>hardboard |
| Roof Section: | 304 x 84 x 3mm<br>(12 x 3⁵/₁₆ x ⅛in)<br>hardboard |
| Roof Locating Strips (4): | 60 x 230mm<br>(2⅜ x 9³/₈in) quadrant |

**Sign**

| | |
|---|---|
| Sign: | 120 x 32 x 6mm<br>(4¾ x 1¼ x ¼in)<br>plywood |
| Stand: | 40 x 40 x 6mm<br>(1⁹/₁₆ x 1⁹/₁₆ x ¼in)<br>plywood |

**Petrol Pumps**

| | |
|---|---|
| Pumps (3): | 35 x 20 x 12mm<br>(1⅜ x ²⁵/₃₂ x ½in)<br>plywood |
| Base: | 110 x 32 x 6mm<br>(4 x 1¼ x ¼in) |

## Construction

Before assembling the walls of each building, cut out all the windows and doors. The walls are simply glued and pinned together (use 20mm (¾in) panel pins) to form the structures as illustrated in the plans and photographs.

Note that the interior wall of the car sales showroom/shop has a door in it that is identical in placement to the door of the exterior wall, but has no window (see **Fig 16.1**).

After assembly, the top edges of the front and back walls (6mm (¼in) plywood) of the car sales showroom/shop and the car body repair/spray booth buildings (see **Fig 16.3**) need to be planed to match the slope of the roof. Use a block plane for this task.

The hardboard roofs are retained by strips of 9mm (⅜in) quadrant. Each roof section has a strip glued to each end so that, when in position, the lengthways face of each piece of quadrant is in contact with the inside of the side walls. Thus the bottom end of each quadrant strip rests against a front/back wall of a building.

To ensure that the two roof sections of both the sales showroom/shop and the workshop (see **Fig 16.4**) align correctly at their apexes, plane the top edge of the shorter section so that when butted together in position they join neatly.

Slot and glue the garage sign into its base (see **Fig 16.5**).

*Fig 16.1*

**Car showroom and shop.**

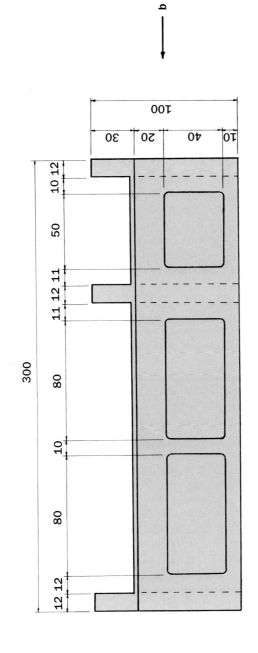

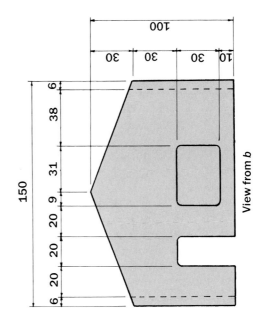

View from b

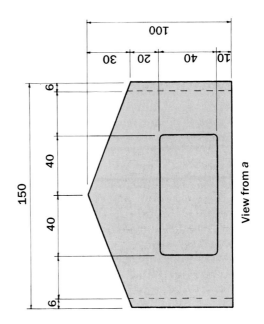

View from a

- Roof removed for clarity
- All window and door corners have
  3mm radii

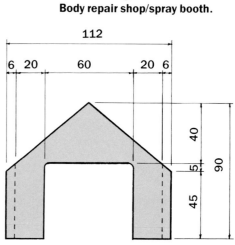

Fig 16.3
**Body repair shop/spray booth.**

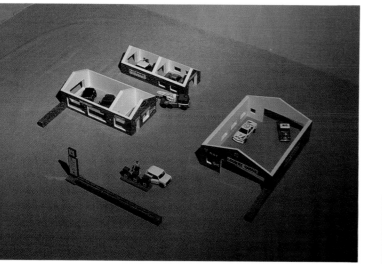

Fig 16.2
**An interior view of Loader's Garage.**

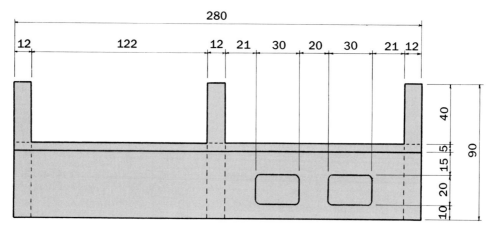

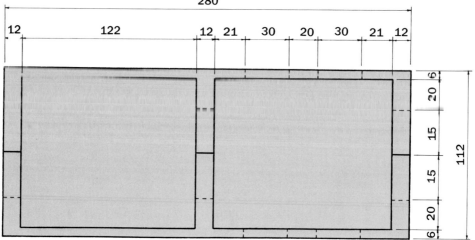

- Roof removed for clarity
- Door and window corners are rounded
  to 3mm (⅛in) radii

- Roof removed for clarity
- Window and door corners rounded to
  3mm (⅛in) radii

*Fig 16.4*
**The workshop.**

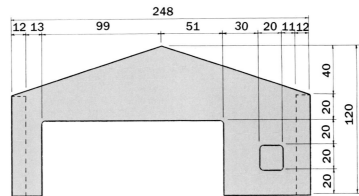

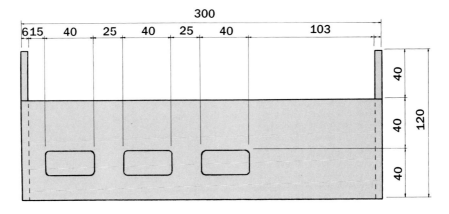

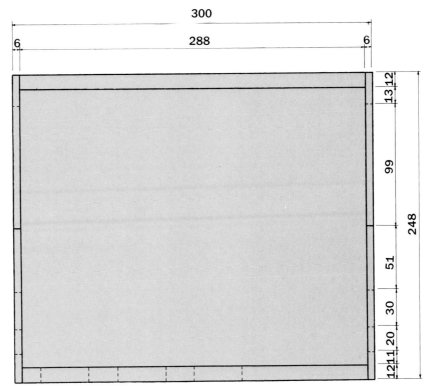

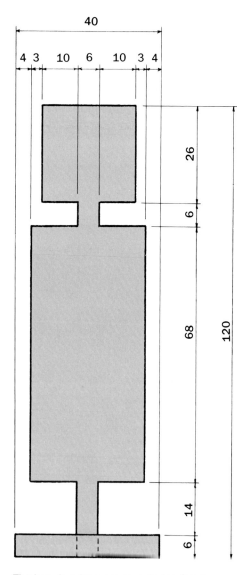

The base's edges are rounded to 3mm
(⅛in) radii

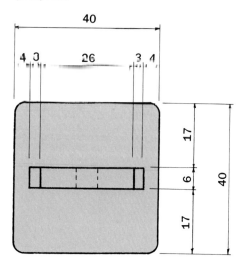

Glue the cut out petrol pumps to their base
(see **Fig 16.6**).

Any suitable lengths of scrap timber may be
used to make the freestanding walls. Make
them to the dimensions of your choice.

## Finishing

Brickwork and tile-finishing paper (the type
used for dolls' houses) were used on Loader's
Garage. These can be obtained from most
good hobbyist suppliers. Alternatively, you
may paint or decorate your garage in your
own way.

Do name your garage to suit the child/children
who will be using it! Children love to have
their own name on the proprietor's board. We
devised our own petrol brand: Blue Star. You
may like to ask the child/children for whom the
garage is intended to design their own
corporate logo.

*Fig 16.5*
**The garage sign and base.**

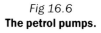
*Fig 16.6*
**The petrol pumps.**

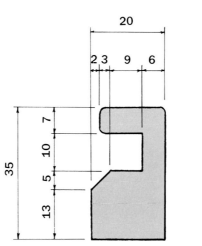

The three rounded edges on the top section of each pump have 1.5mm (¹⁄₁₆in) radii

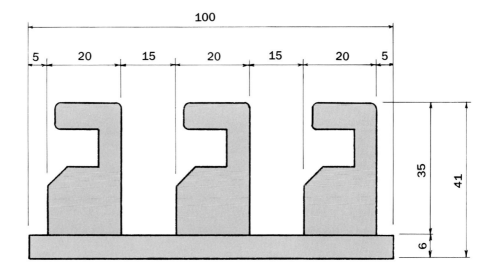

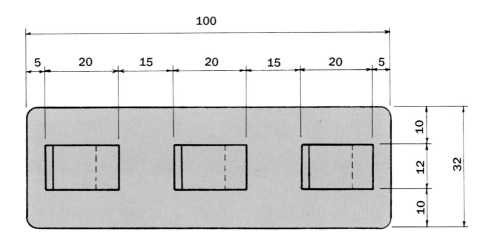

# SEVENTEEN

# Marvellous Mighty Mervyn

This is a simple magic trick in which Marvellous Mighty Mervyn, the escapologist, mysteriously disappears from a locked and bound strongbox!

The trick is primarily intended to entertain preschool children. It is simple to operate and is therefore suitable for older children to perform.

## Effect

1 The magician introduces Marvellous Mighty Mervyn, the escapologist, to the audience. He shows them that Mervyn's feet have been secured to a solid base.

2 The door of the strongbox is opened, revealing the empty box.

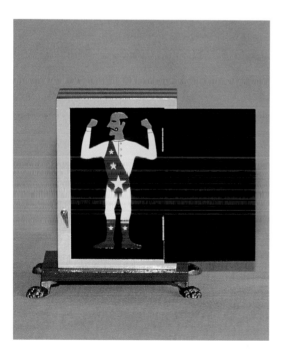

3 Mervyn is placed inside.

4 The magician locks the door and places a sack (or bag) over the strongbox.

The strongbox (now inside the bag) is lifted from its stand into the air. To totally disorientate Mervyn, the magician spins the bag and strongbox together several times. The strongbox is then taken from the sack and placed back upon the stand.

The bag is removed and given to the audience to verify that it is empty.

5  The magician undoes the catch on the strongbox and opens the door. Miraculously, Marvellous Mighty Mervyn has vanished!

6  The magician then points to a shelf (mantelpiece or bookcase, etc.) behind the audience and, lo and behold, there is Mervyn himself, striking a pose!

## Set-up and operation

Prior to the audience assembling, place or hide (depending on how observant your audience is) one of the Mervyns on a shelf. This should be behind the audience during the illusion.

Place the stand, with the strongbox on it, onto your performance surface/table.

Ensure that there is not a direct light source hitting the interior of the strongbox when its door is opened. If the illusion is to be performed during the day, set the trick up with a room window behind you and the audience in front of you. These precautions are necessary to help disguise the secret partition in the strongbox.

Introduce Mervyn to the audience and show them that he is securely attached to his base.

Unfasten the strongbox's catch and open the door. Without removing it from its stand show how the box is empty.

Carefully place Mervyn fully into the box, ensuring that the back of his base slides smoothly into the gap at the bottom of the secret partition. (Candle wax rubbed onto Mervyn's base before undertaking the trick can help lubricate the base.)

Shut the strongbox and fasten the catch.

Show the empty bag to the audience and ask them to inspect it. Then place the bag over the strongbox, covering it completely. The bag should be inconspicuously marked in some way. This mark should be FACING YOU, the magician. This is to indicate the back of the strongbox.

Turn the bag and covered strongbox in the air a few times. Explain to the audience that this is to disorientate and hinder Mervyn in his escape attempt.

Take the strongbox out of the bag, but make sure that the back door (the one that opens to reveal the empty compartment) is FACING THE AUDIENCE when it is placed back onto the stand. The inconspicuous mark on the bag will aid you in this.

Pass the bag to the audience so that they can verify that it is still an ordinary empty bag.

Unfasten the strongbox catch and open the door.

The strongbox appears to be empty!

Dramatically point or indicate to where the other, previously placed/hidden Mervyn is.

Bow to the audience's amazed applause!

## Performance notes

When performing this illusion, your manner of speech, or patter, is important. You, the magician, are in essence promoting Marvellous Mighty Mervyn. Remember that your audience, whatever their age, wants to be entertained. However good the trick or illusion is, it is the manner and style in which it is performed that makes it entertaining! You must be confident and rehearsed. Really 'sell' the illusion and try and inject some humour.

A key element of the illusion is the hiding or placing of the second Mervyn. It is vital that he remains undiscovered until the appropriate moment. It is a nice touch if Mervyn is discovered peeping from behind an object. If this is not possible then the aid of an accomplice may be necessary. He should have Mervyn concealed in a pocket and secretly placed in a prominent position BEHIND the audience. This task can be undertaken when the attention of the audience is on the main illusion.

The positioning of the illusion in relation to the room's light source has already been mentioned, but to aid the performance the audience should be situated a few feet away.

---

### CUTTING LIST

*(All from birch plywood)*

**Strongbox**

| | |
|---|---|
| Side (2): | 104 x 46 x 10mm |
| | ($4^3/_{32}$ x $1^{13}/_{16}$ x $^3/_8$in) |
| Top and Base (2): | 84 x 46 x 6mm |
| | ($3^5/_{16}$ x $1^{13}/_{16}$ x $^1/_4$in) |
| Partition: | 100 x 70 x 1.5mm |
| | (4 x $2^3/_4$ x $^1/_{16}$in) |
| Doors (2): | 104 x 64 x 12mm |
| | ($4^3/_{32}$ x $2^{17}/_{32}$ x $^1/_2$in) |
| Stand: | (104 x 66 x 6mm) |
| | $4^3/_{32}$ x $2^5/_8$ x $^1/_4$in) |

**Marvellous Mighty Mervyn**

| | |
|---|---|
| Bases (2): | 64 x 25 x 3mm |
| | ($2^{17}/_{32}$ x 1 x $^1/_8$in) |
| Mervyns: | small quantity of 3mm |
| | ($^1/_8$in) plywood |

**Miscellaneous**

(4) 16mm (⅝in) brass butt hinges
(2) decorative upholstery nails (for door
    handles)
(2) turnbuttons (for catches)
(4) claw feet

---

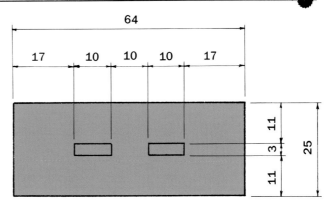

3mm (⅛in) thick

*Fig 17.2*
**Mervyn's base.**

## Construction

### Marvellous Mighty Mervyn

Copy Mervyn's profile onto prepared 3mm (⅛in) plywood and cut out two Mervyns (see **Fig. 17.1**). If you wish you could cut these out in one operation by pinning two pieces of 3mm (⅛in) plywood together. After cutting remove the pins and fill the pin holes with filler.

Cut out the two stands (see **Fig 17.2**). Centralize each Mervyn onto its respective stand's surface and, with a sharp pencil, mark around the feet 'tenons'. Using a fretsaw, cut out two slots on each stand. Glue each Mervyn to his stand. When the glue is set, clean up any unevenness on the underside using a block plane and/or abrasive paper.

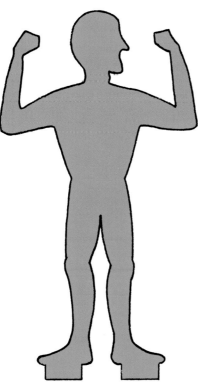

3mm (⅛in) thick

*Fig 17.1*
**Mervyn (full-size scale).**

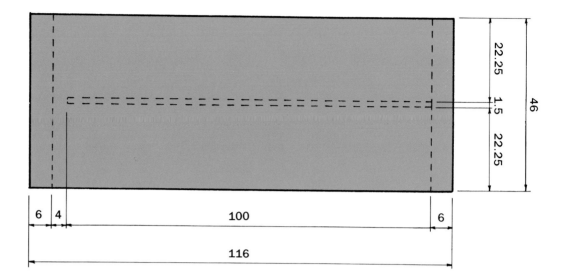

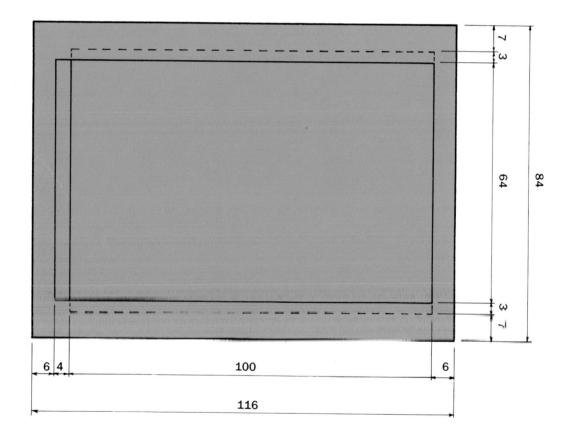

Fig 17.3
**Strongbox (front and side views).**

The strongbox is drawn with its doors
removed for clarity

## The strongbox

Cut out and prepare all the components (see **Fig 17.3**). Before assembling, a vertical slot is cut in each inside face of the side pieces. Cut these with a tenon saw to a depth of 3mm (⅛in) while holding each side securely in a vice. The central secret partition fits into these slots. If the fit proves too tight, chamfer the edges of the partition.

Glue the partition into place, remembering to leave a gap at the bottom. This gap must be large enough to enable Mervyn's base to just slide underneath when the illusion is performed.

Glue and pin the top and bottom pieces onto the sides of the strongbox.

16mm (⅝in) brass butt hinges were used to fix the doors into position. Due to the thin width of the doors these hinges were fitted flat on the outside. Fancy shaped hinges could be used instead if desired.

Two small brass turnbuttons are used as catches to secure the doors (one per door), and decorative upholstery nails are used as the handles. It is best to fit these after the strongbox has been painted.

## The stand

The stand is simply a piece of 6mm (¼in) plywood with four claw feet situated at each corner. These are screwed into position on the underside of the plywood once the stand has been painted.

## Finishing

Marvellous Mighty Mervyn should be painted in a striking, eyecatching fashion. This is so that he will attract the audience's attention and will contrast against the black interior of the strongbox. It is important that his base is painted matt black.

Make the two Mervyns' facial features bold. Remember that the audience will be viewing him from a few feet away. Also, bold and simple facial features are easier to duplicate – the whole illusion is ruined if the two Mervyns are not identical!

The painting and colour scheme of the strongbox is crucial. The interior, including the inside of the doors MUST BE PAINTED MATT BLACK. A dead matt black finish will not reflect light, making the secret partition virtually invisible and disguising the true interior dimensions of both interior compartments.

The exterior of the strongbox should be brightly decorated (to help distract the audience), but care should be taken not to over-elaborate.

An important painting note is that the strongbox must look exactly the same, whether viewed from the front or the back. Therefore the doors must be identical – the audience must believe that there is only ONE door.

Fit the door handles, hinges and catches when finishing is complete.

Finish the stand in a style of your own choosing.

# EIGHTEEN

# Monster Pick-ups

**T**he inspiration for these toys is drawn from those extraordinary, powerful American vehicles that have enormous wheels.

Although primarily push-along toys, each of our monster pick-ups can be attached to a cord and winch. Placed side by side they can race each other (winched along) over various obstacles (such as blocks of wood, old books, cushions etc.), just like their gigantic real-life counterparts!

## CUTTING LIST – PICK-UPS

*(All birch plywood)*

| | |
|---|---|
| Side body pieces (2): | 200 x 52 x 3mm (8 x 2$^{1}$/$_{16}$ x $^{1}$/$_{8}$in) |
| Chassis: | 200 x 74 x 12mm (8 x 2$^{15}$/$_{16}$ x $^{1}$/$_{2}$in) |
| Back panel of cab: | 74 x 40 x 6mm (2$^{15}$/$_{16}$ x 1$^{9}$/$_{16}$ x $^{1}$/$_{4}$in) |
| Roll bar holder (2): | 74 x 10 x 10mm (2$^{15}$/$_{16}$ x $^{3}$/$_{8}$ x $^{3}$/$_{8}$in) |
| Bonnet block piece: | 74 x 68 x 18mm (2$^{15}$/$_{16}$ x 2$^{11}$/$_{16}$ x $^{3}$/$_{4}$in) |
| Cab seat: | 74 x 20 x 10mm (2$^{15}$/$_{16}$ x $^{25}$/$_{32}$ x $^{3}$/$_{8}$in) |
| Bumper (2): | 86 x 10 x 3mm (3$^{13}$/$_{32}$ x $^{3}$/$_{8}$ x $^{1}$/$_{8}$in) |
| Side bumper (4): | 14 x 10 x 3mm ($^{9}$/$_{16}$ x $^{3}$/$_{8}$ x $^{1}$/$_{8}$in) |
| Cab roof: | 80 x 43 x 1.5mm (3$^{5}$/$_{32}$ x 1$^{11}$/$_{16}$ x $^{1}$/$_{16}$in) |
| Tailgate: | 74 x 19 x 6mm (2$^{15}$/$_{16}$ x $^{3}$/$_{4}$ x $^{1}$/$_{4}$in) |
| Rollbar: | 68 x 52 x 3mm (2$^{11}$/$_{16}$ x 2$^{1}$/$_{16}$ x $^{1}$/$_{8}$in) |
| Axle rod retainer (side piece) (4): | 70 x 50 x 6mm (2$^{3}$/$_{4}$ x 2 x $^{1}$/$_{4}$in) |
| Axle rod retainer (centre block) (2): | 62 x 50 x 18mm 2$^{15}$/$_{32}$ x 2 x $^{3}$/$_{4}$in) |

**Miscellaneous**
6mm (*$^{1}$/$_{4}$in*) steel axle rod
(4) spring hubcaps (8 for 8 wheeler)
(4) 100mm (*4in*) wheels (8 for 8 wheeler)
(4) washers to fit axle rod
screw eyelet

## CUTTING LIST – WINCH

| | |
|---|---|
| Base: | 150 x 100 x 12mm (6 x 4 x $^{1}$/$_{2}$in) plywood |
| Uprights (2): | 112 x 100 x 6mm (4$^{1}$/$_{2}$ x 4 x $^{1}$/$_{4}$in) plywood |
| Discs (2): | 120mm (4$^{3}$/$_{4}$in) diameter x 6mm ($^{1}$/$_{4}$in) thick plywood |
| Centre rod: | 122mm (4$^{13}$/$_{16}$in) long x 18mm ($^{3}$/$_{4}$in) diameter dowel |
| Handle connection: | 66 x 28 x 6mm (2$^{5}$/$_{8}$ x 1$^{1}$/$_{8}$ x $^{1}$/$_{4}$in) plywood |
| Handle: | 40mm (1$^{5}$/$_{8}$in) long x 6mm ($^{1}$/$_{4}$in) diameter dowel |
| Centre rod end disc: | 28mm (1$^{1}$/$_{8}$in) diameter x 3mm ($^{1}$/$_{8}$in) thick plywood |

**Miscellaneous**
Length of cord/string
Small hook

## Construction

**Tip** When cutting out the side body pieces (see **Fig 18.1**), pin two pieces of 3mm ($^{1}$/$_{8}$in) plywood together and cut them, using a fretsaw, in one operation. Remember to leave the pins standing proud so they can be removed easily.

Glue and pin the bonnet block (see **Fig 18.2**) in position on the chassis as shown in Fig 18.3.

Fretsaw the rear window out of the rear panel of the cab, then glue and pin it to the cab seat.

Glue and pin the side body panels onto the sides of the chassis/bonnet block (see

Fig 18.3). Slightly round the edges of the bonnet to produce a less angular look.

Fix the seat and rear cab panel assembly into position.

Fit the tailgate.

Glue the roof of the cab and the bumper into place.

Before fitting the rollbar holders, drill the required hole in each of them (see **Fig 18.2**). The rollbars are fitted 'dry' (not glued) when each pick-up has been painted. This is so that they may be replaced easily should they break after a severe roll. For this reason a round, rather than square, location hole is used.

The rollbars must fit firmly, but not tightly, into these holes. A 5.5mm (7/32in) drill bit should be approximately the right size. See Fig 18.4 for the dimensions of the rollbar.

Each axle rod holder (see **Fig 18.5**) is constructed from two shaped plywood sides which are glued and pinned to a plywood block. Before assembly, drill the axle rod holes into the sides. Also, as the holders are glued and screwed to the underside of the chassis, it is advisable to drill and countersink two screw holes in each plywood block before assembling.

Plane the plywood blocks to size after the plywood sides have been fitted. (We found a block plane most suitable for this task.)

Fit the wheels after the pick-ups have been painted. The pick-up *Oddball* has been fitted with eight wheels and will therefore need a longer axle rod than the *Ghoul*.

If you intend to use the pick-ups with the winch, screw a small eyelet to the block of the front axle rod retainer assembly.

## Finishing

Bear in mind that children will love to play with these toys out on the lawn or in the back yard, so an elaborate paint finish is not necessary. However, try to achieve an overall finish that is complementary to these contemporary vehicles!

## Winch construction

**Tip** Before cutting out the handle connecting piece, drill out the holes for the centre rod and the handle (see **Fig 18.6**).

When all the components have been cut out and prepared, drill the holes in the uprights and the discs. Note that the holes in the uprights must allow the centre rod to rotate freely, but the disc holes must allow the centre rod to fit snugly.

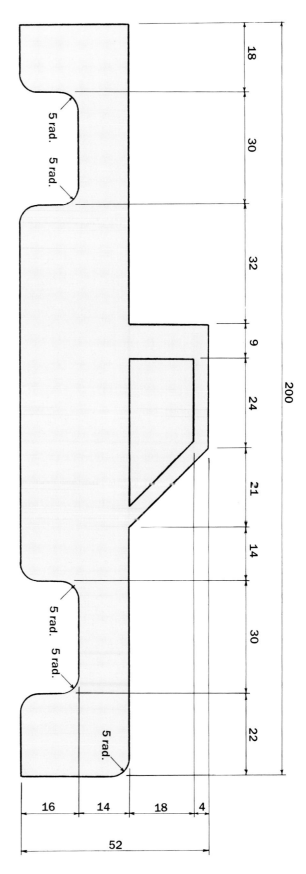

*Fig 18.1*
**Side body piece.**

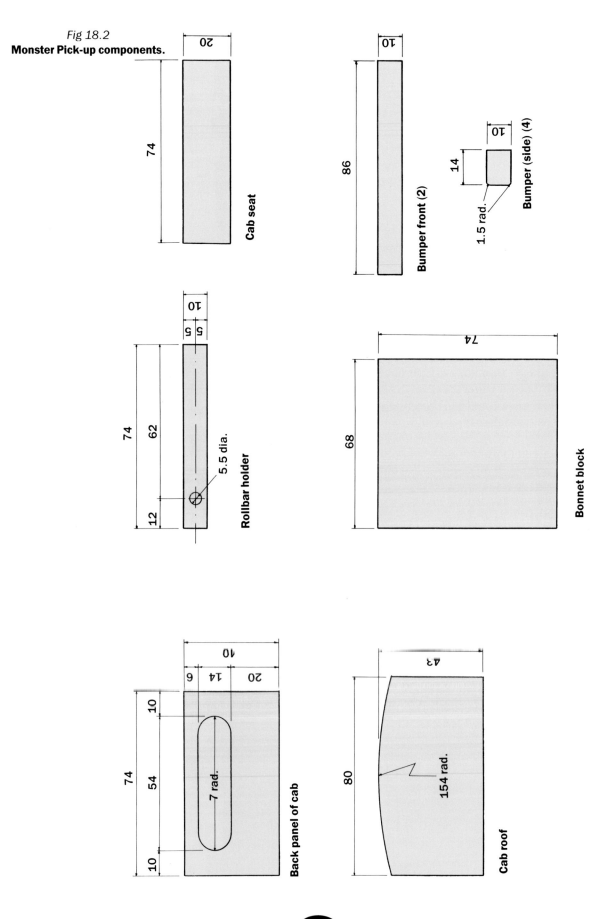

*Fig 18.2*
**Monster Pick-up components.**

Cab seat

Bumper front (2)

Bumper (side) (4)

Rollbar holder

Bonnet block

Back panel of cab

Cab roof

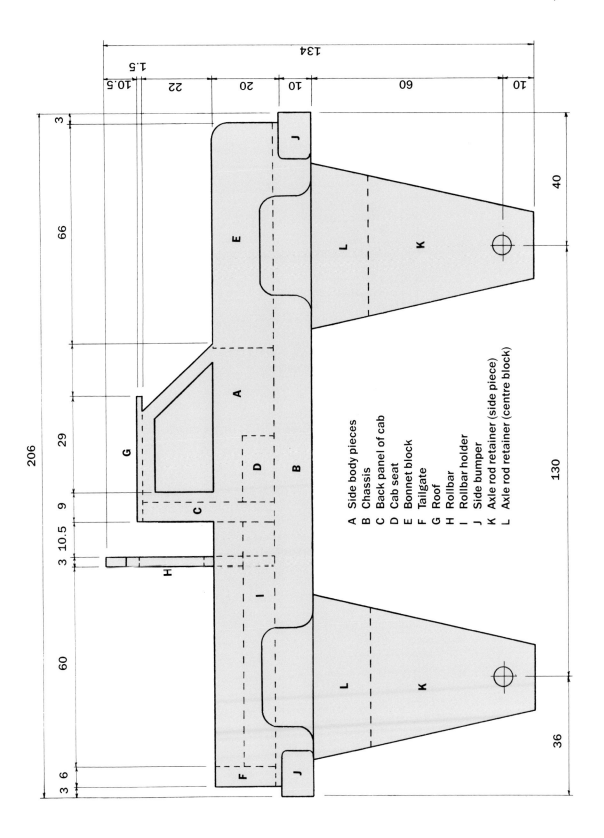

Fig 18.3
**Side view illustrating components' arrangement.**

A  Side body pieces
B  Chassis
C  Back panel of cab
D  Cab seat
E  Bonnet block
F  Tailgate
G  Roof
H  Rollbar
I  Rollbar holder
J  Side bumper
K  Axle rod retainer (side piece)
L  Axle rod retainer (centre block)

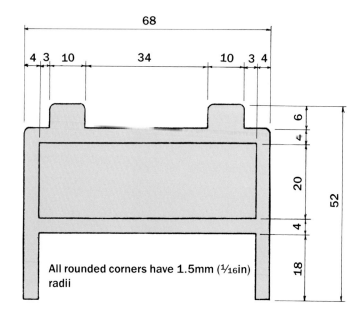

Fig 18.4 (a)
**The rollbar.**

All rounded corners have 1.5mm (¹⁄₁₆in) radii

Fig 18.4 (b)
**Plan view of rollbar holder.**

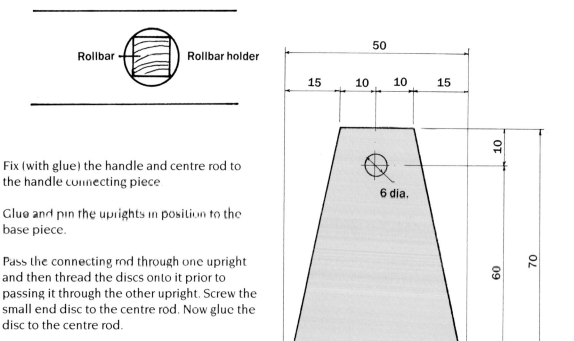

Rollbar — Rollbar holder

Fix (with glue) the handle and centre rod to the handle connecting piece.

Glue and pin the uprights in position to the base piece.

Pass the connecting rod through one upright and then thread the discs onto it prior to passing it through the other upright. Screw the small end disc to the centre rod. Now glue the disc to the centre rod.

Wind as much cord as you require onto the winch and tie a hook to the end. We fashioned our hook out of a link of brass chain. You will need a junior hacksaw to cut through the link and round-nosed pliers to bend it to shape.

6 dia.

Fig 18.5
**The axle rod retainer (side piece).**

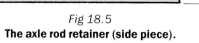

**Base**

150

100

10 rad.

10 rad.

10 rad.

10 rad.

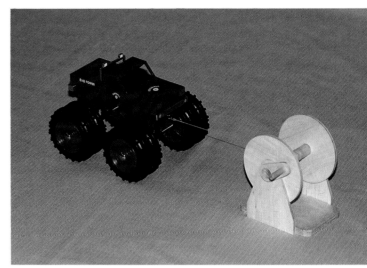

Fig 18.7
**The winch mechanism in operation.**

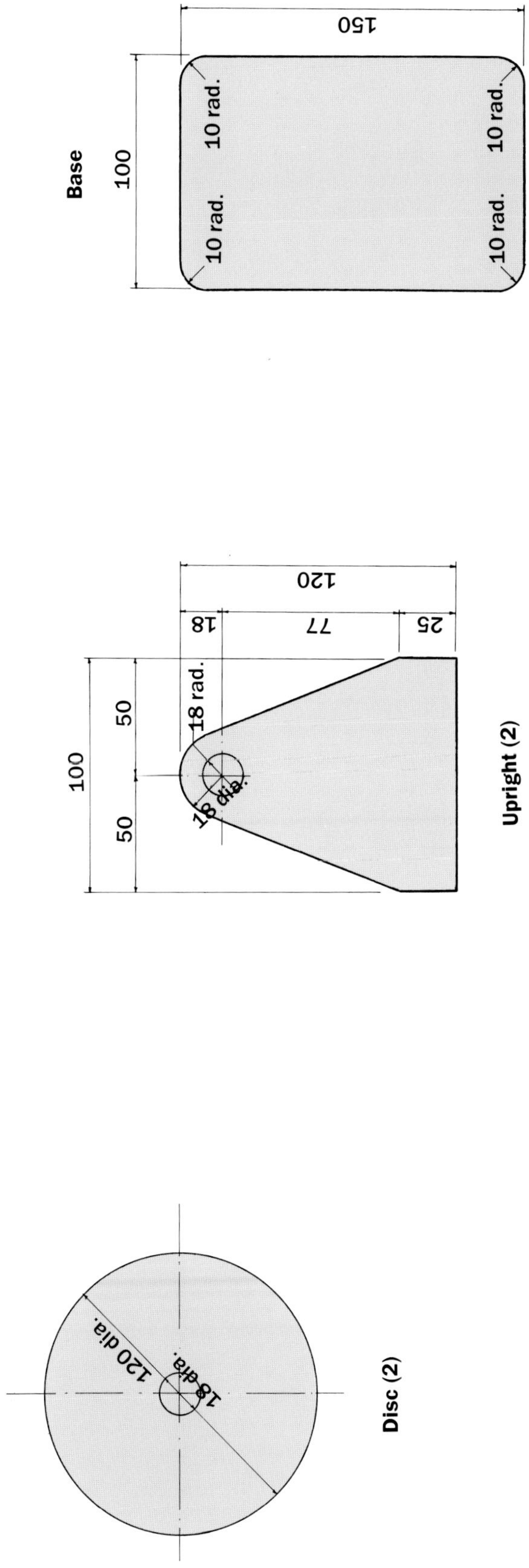

**Upright (2)**

120

18

77

25

18 rad.

100

50

50

18 dia.

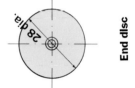

28 dia.

**End disc**

**Disc (2)**

120 dia.

18 dia.

**Handle connecting piece**

66

15

40

11

10 dia.

18 dia.

15 rad.

11 rad.

Fig 18.6
**Winch components.**

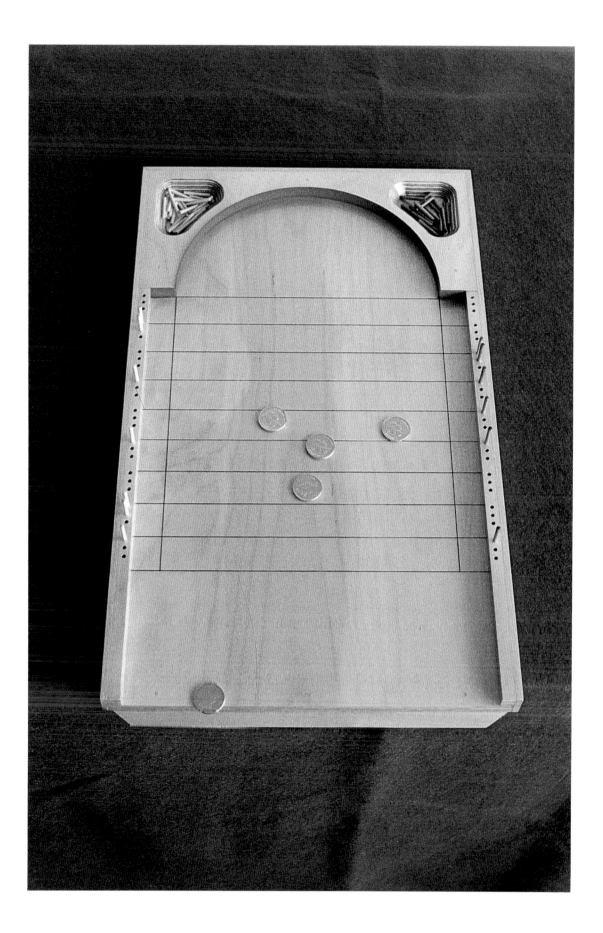

# NINETEEN

# Shove Ha'penny

Shove Ha'penny has been played, primarily in public houses, for centuries. Unfortunately its appeal has waned somewhat in recent years, and now it is becoming increasingly rare to see a game taking place. This may be due to the introduction of video and slot machines. Placed next to these 'wonders of the technological age' the humble Shove Ha'penny board may seem rather drab to some.

This is a great shame, any newcomer to this game will soon appreciate the tremendous skill required to play. It is also great fun!

In our version of the game new ten-pence pieces (24mm ($^{15}/_{16}$in) diameter coins) have been substituted for the old ha'pennies. There's inflation for you!

*Fig 19.1*
**The board.**

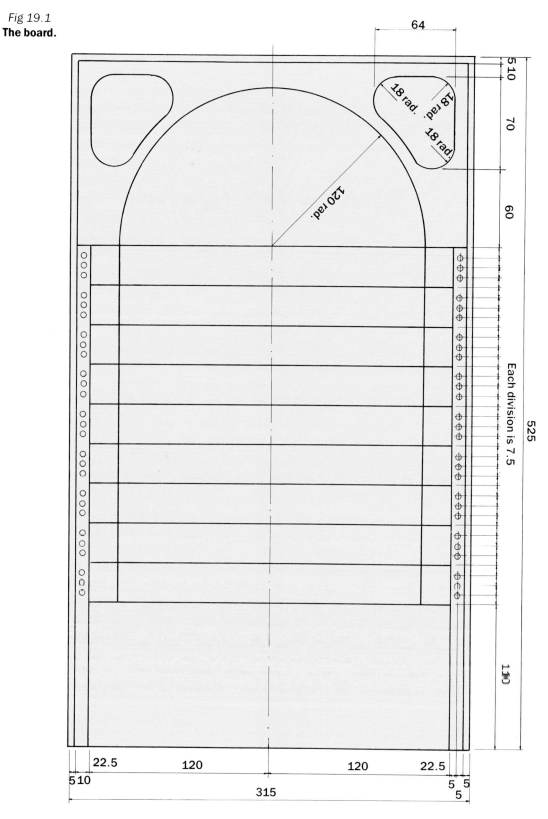

64

510

70

60

120 rad.

18 rad.

18 rad.

18 rad.

525

Each division is 7.5

130

22.5    120              120          22.5

510                                        5  5
                                           5

315

• All peg holes are 3.3mm (⅛in) in
  diameter and 6mm (¼in) in depth

• The peg storage dishes are drawn
  showing 90° sides

## CUTTING LIST

| | |
|---|---|
| Playing board: | 520 x 305 x 12mm (20⅛ x 12 x ½in) birch plywood |
| Top end piece: | 305 x 140 x 12mm (12 x 5½ x ½in) birch plywood |
| Side scoring wall (2): | 380 x 10 x 12mm (15 x ⅜ x ½in) birch plywood |
| Bottom end retaining piece (1): | 300 x 30 x 18mm (11¹³⁄₁₆ x 1³⁄₁₆ x ¾n) hardwood |
| Side edging (2): | 525 x 25 x 5mm (20⁵⁄₁₆ x 1 x ³⁄₁₆in) ramin strip |
| Top end edging: | 315 x 25 x 5mm (12⁷⁄₁₆ x 1 x ³⁄₁₆in) ramin strip |
| Scoring peg (54) | 25 x 3mm (1 x ⅛in) diameter dowel |

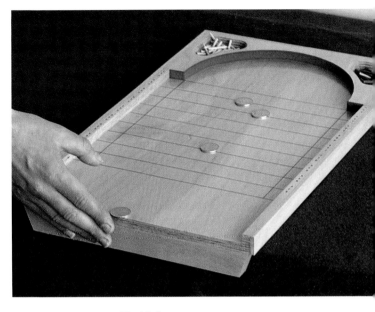

*Fig 19.2*
**The bottom retaining piece.**

## Construction

Use a fretsaw or a bandsaw to cut the large rebound curve on the top end piece (see **Fig 19.1**). The two dishes (for peg storage) are cut by setting the cutting table of a fretsaw machine to an angle of 40°. Should this be a problem for your machine, or if you do not own a machine, cut the dishes out at 90° instead.

Glue and pin the top end piece to the main playing board. Mark the ten bed dividing lines and two side lines. Use a black Biro and rule for this task. Frequently wipe the Biro nib on a scrap piece of paper to keep it from smudging.

Cut and prepare the two side scoring strips. Then drill the 27 scoring peg holes in each one. Use a drill bit the diameter of which will allow the 3mm (⅛in) pegs to be put in and taken out easily. We found a 3.3mm diameter drill bit to be perfect for our dowel pegs. Drill these scoring peg holes to a depth of 6mm (¼in).

Edging may now be applied. We used 25 x 5mm (1 x ³⁄₁₆in) ramin strip, but you may use a style of edging to your own choosing.

Prepare a piece of hardwood (we used sycamore) for the bottom retaining piece. This will butt against a table edge during play. Glue and pin this into position, underneath the front edge of the game board (see **Fig 19.2**).

Varnish the game board, giving it at least four coats.

When the varnish has dried, test out the slide factor of the board. Simply tap some ten-pence pieces up the board. If they do not slide smoothly you can rectify this by waxing the playing surface. Apply the wax using grade 0000 wire wool.

Apply the velour to the curved rebound wall.

Cut the 54 pegs from ramin dowel. It is easier to colour/stain the dark pegs before cutting them out.

## Shove Ha'penny

### Equipment

- Shove Ha'penny board
- 27 white scoring pegs
- 27 dark scoring pegs
- 5 new ten-pence pieces (24mm (¹⁵⁄₁₆in) diameter coins)

**Fig 19.3**
**The coin protrudes over the edge of the playing board.**

## Object of the game

By means of shoving the coins up the board each player must try to land a coin three times in each horizontal band (called a 'bed'). The first to do so is the winner.

## Play *(for two players)*

The board is placed on a table with its bottom retaining piece butted up against the edge of the table. This will help ensure that the board will remain stable during play.

**Fig 19.4**
**End elevation, showing bottom retaining piece.**

Place the five coins alongside, but not onto, the board. Place all the white pegs into one of the end dishes and the dark ones into the other.

Players must toss a coin to determine who gets which colour. The player who wins the toss scores the white pegs and starts the game.

He begins by placing a coin so it is protruding over the front edge of the playing board (**Fig 19.3**). Then he must strike the coin with his hand in order to slide the coin up the board. The intention is to land the coin in one of the nine horizontal zones. If successful, it scores, but if it rests on one of the black lines, it does not.

Coins may be knocked into scoring positions by another coin. Conversely a scoring coin that is knocked onto a black line does not score.

When the player has shoved all five coins into play then (and only then), is his score calculated. Place a peg in a hole that corresponds with a bed that has a scoring coin or coins in it. Each player must only score in the peg holes directly in line with their storage dish.

It is now the turn of the next player. Play is continued in this manner until a player has pegged three times in each bed. He is the winner of the game.

The beds may be scored in any order. However, once a player has pegged one bed

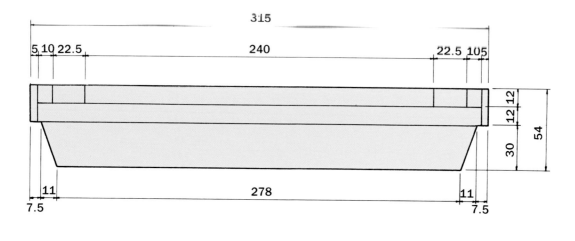

three times, any further scoring coins for that bed are credited to the opposing player. If the opposing player already has three pegs in that bed then the coin is ignored.

If one coin ends up lying on top of another, neither coin scores. Coins that land more than halfway over a side line are removed from play for that player's particular turn. A coin that is not more than halfway over a side line may remain on the board, but does not score unless knocked into a scoring position by another coin.

The rebounding of coins, either from the curved back wall or side walls is permitted.

If, when shoved, a coin does not reach the first line, the shot may be retaken. However, if a coin strikes another coin that is resting on the first line, the shot may not be retaken, although it may be knocked into play by another coin.

## Play alternatives

If at first you find the use of ten-pence-sized coins too difficult you could use smaller diameter coins, such as one- or five-pence coins instead.

If a shorter game is required, peg each bed only twice instead of three times.

TWENTY

# Skittle Alley Skittlers

**B**ring the fun of the pub game to your home table top!

As in the full-sized game, the skill of the players decides the outcome. Careful eye-to-hand coordination is required to operate the small toy skittlers successfully.

Two versions of skittles have been designed, one for left-handed use and one for right-handed use. The toy skittler that bowls with his left hand is for right-handed players and the skittler that bowls with his right hand is for left-handed players.

## CUTTING LIST

**Alley**

| | |
|---|---|
| Base piece: | 550 x 164 x 6mm $(21^{21}/_{32}$ x $6^{15}/_{32}$ x $^1/_4$in) plywood |
| Gutter piece: | 500 x 164 x 6mm $(19^{11}/_{16}$ x $6^{15}/_{32}$ x $^1/_4$in) plywood |
| Playing surface: | 500 x 120 x 10mm $(19^{11}/_{16}$ x $4^3/_4$ x $^3/_8$in) plywood |
| Back stop: | 164 x 51 x 10mm $(6^{15}/_{32}$ x 2 x $^3/_8$in) plywood |
| Edging strip (2): | 556 x 22 x 6mm $(21^7/_8$ x $^7/_8$ x $^1/_4$in) hardwood strip |
| (2): | 176 x 22 x 6mm $(6^{15}/_{16}$ x $^7/_8$ x $^1/_4$in) hardwood strip |

**Skittles (9)**
25 x 10mm *(1 x $^3/_8$in)* diameter dowel

**Skittlers**
Small amount of 6mm *($^1/_4$in)* plywood
Small amount of 3mm *($^1/_8$in)* plywood

*Fig 20.1*
**Parts of a skittler:** *(a)* **body,** *(b)* **arms,** *(c)* **base and** *(d)* **handle.**

A

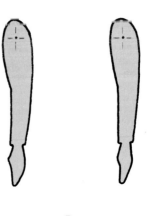

B

## Construction

### Skittler *(right-handed use)*

Transfer the drawing of the skittler onto 6mm ($^1/_4$in) birch plywood, and the drawings of the arms, base and handle onto 3mm ($^1/_8$in) birch plywood (see **Fig 20.1**).

It is best to drill the shoulder and arm holes before cutting out the components of the skittler. The size of these holes will be dictated by the actual diameter of the 3mm ($^1/_8$in) dowel used to attach the arms, as one piece of dowel of the same size as another tends to vary greatly. The skittlers shown have their arm holes drilled with a 3.3mm bit, and their bodies with a 3.5mm bit so as to allow free rotation of the arms when assembled.

After all the holes have been drilled, cut out all the parts with a fretsaw.

Thoroughly sand all the components using progressively finer grades of abrasive paper.

Glue a length of 3mm ($^1/_8$in) diameter dowel into one of the armholes. Its length should be slightly longer than both the arms and body width put together, thereby allowing free movement of the arms when assembled and painted.

Glue the skittler's body and the handle into position on the base.

When the glue has set, remove any unevenness on the underside of the base.

Paint the body, base and inside of the skittler's arms.

With the painting complete, the skittler's arms may be assembled. Pass the dowel connected to one arm through the body via the shoulder hole. Attach, with glue, the other arm. Before the glue dries, the arms should be set as follows:

**1** Place the bowling arm to the point where it would make contact with a ball, usually just in front of the skittler's front foot.
**2** Now move the other arm to a position slightly in front of his head.

When the glue has set, paint the unpainted parts of the arms.

A piece of velour is applied to the underside of the skittler's base.

## Skittler (left-handed use)

Follow the instructions above for right-handed use, but reverse the base before the skittler is attached. The front foot cutaway is then on the right side of the base.

## Skittles

Cut nine 25mm (1in) long skittles from a length of sanded 10mm (³⁄₈in) ramin dowel.

## Skittle balls

We used three 19mm (¾in) diameter wood balls. Sometimes you can obtain these partly drilled. While lining up a shot, place the ball on its drilled hole to help it remain steady on the alley surface. If the balls you use are not drilled and they will not sit still on the alley, then you can drill them yourself.

Do not worry if your skittle balls are not entirely spherical. This can actually help simulate the real game, as few pubs have perfectly round skittle balls or level alleys!

## The alley

Cut out and prepare all the components (see **Fig 20.2**).

The alley's playing surface is made from 10mm (³⁄₈in) birch plywood. This is glued, centrally, onto the gutter piece, a piece of 6mm (¼in) birch plywood that is the same length as the alley playing surface, but wider. This in turn is glued to the base piece, which consists of 6mm (¼in) plywood.

The backstop of the end gutter is glued and pinned into position. With this done, the edging is glued and pinned into position. Mitre the corners at the skittler's end if desired.

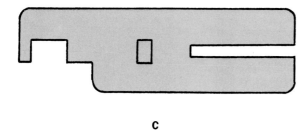

C

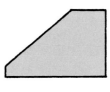

D

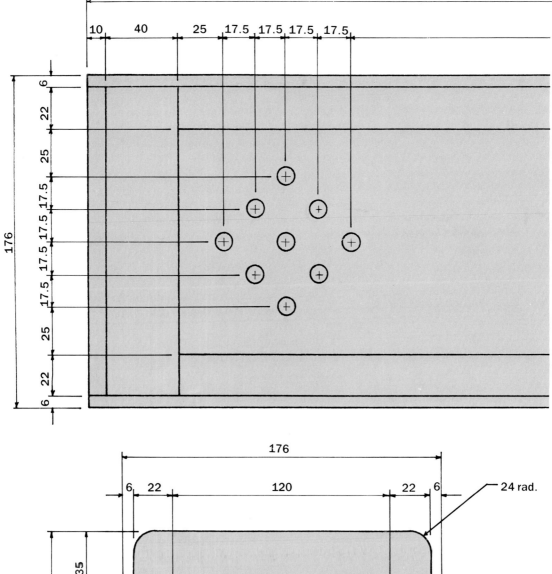

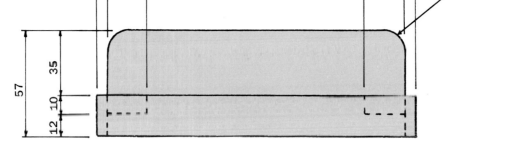

Fig 20.2
**Plan and end view of the skittle alley.**

The bowling line and skittle placings are drawn using a Biro. Use a circle template to help you mark the 10mm (³⁄₈in) skittle placings.

Varnish, paint and decorate the alley as desired.

**Operating the skittler**

The directions given are for right-handed use. Please reverse for left-handed use.

Place the skittler onto the alley behind the

556

315                                                                    90        6

bowling line, and face him towards the skittles.
Situate a ball just in front of him. The ball may
be placed on the line or behind it, never in
front. Shot direction is determined by moving
the skittler by using his handle (see **Fig 20.3**).

In order to bowl a ball you will need to hold
the skittler's handle steady with your left hand.
Using your right hand, rotate the skittler's arms
until his left hand is directly behind the ball.
Check the alignment of the shot required and
adjust if necessary.

Smoothly pull the skittler's right hand
backwards, thereby making his left hand
stroke the ball down the alley.

With a little practice you should soon be
capable of achieving a variety of shots.

## Skittle alley skittlers

### Object of the game

To knock over as many skittles as possible in

*Fig 20.3*
**The 'throwing' action.**

Fig 20.4
**The skittlers begin a game.**

a given number of 'hands' (three bowls of the ball).

## Preparation

Place the nine skittles onto their marks at the far end of the alley. At the other end, put the skittler onto the alley behind the bowling line. Make sure that the three skittle balls are placed into one of the gutters by the skittler.

Determine the order of play.

Draw up the score sheet, putting the names of the players in the correct order of play.

## Play

Skittles can either be played as an individual or team game. The playing and scoring system is the same for both situations.

Each player has six hands in the game. Each hand consists of the skittler bowling three balls in turn.

Play begins with the first player bowling a ball. The ball must be placed on or behind the bowling line which runs across the alley.

If, before striking a skittle/s, the ball runs into one of the side or end gutters, it is deemed out of play and no points are scored.

Also, if before striking a skittle/s, the ball rebounds out of a gutter and hits over a skittle/s, it is still deemed out of play and no points are scored. Any skittles knocked down in this way are replaced.

If the ball bowled is successful and knocks down a skittle/s, clear these and the ball into the end gutter, but *only* when the ball and knocked over skittles have stopped rolling.

Continuing in this way, the skittler bowls his other two balls, after which his hand is over.

In the event of a player bowling all the skittles over on his first ball (called a flopper) or second ball (called a spare), all the skittles are replaced and he may attempt to knock them down with the remaining ball/s of his hand.

After a player has completed his hand, the score is recorded on the score sheet and the next player plays his first hand. After all the players have skittled their first hand, play returns to the initial player, who now skittles

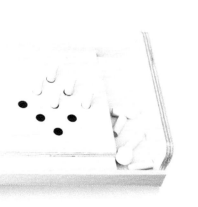

Fig 20.5
**The game during play.**

## Skittles scoresheet

| HOME TEAM | | | | | | | |
|---|---|---|---|---|---|---|---|
| PLAYER | HANDS | | | | | | TOTAL |
| | | | | | | | |
| | | | | | | | |
| | | | | | | | |
| | | | | | | | |
| | | | | | | | |
| GRAND TOTAL | | | | | | | |

| AWAY TEAM | | | | | | | |
|---|---|---|---|---|---|---|---|
| PLAYER | HANDS | | | | | | TOTAL |
| | | | | | | | |
| | | | | | | | |
| | | | | | | | |
| | | | | | | | |
| | | | | | | | |
| GRAND TOTAL | | | | | | | |

his second hand, and so on until all the players have each skittled their six hands.

When playing skittles as a team, play alternates from team to team:

- Player one of team A skittles his first hand.
- Player one of team B skittles his first hand.
- Player two of team A skittles his first hand, and so on.

The winner is the individual or team that has the highest total score at the end of the game.

The game time may be shortened by reducing the number of hands played by each player.

One point is scored for each skittle knocked over.

*Fig 20.6*
**The skittlers in action.**

# TWENTY-ONE

# Yo-Yos

Yo-Yos have been a popular children's toy for many years. With practice and perseverance, many tricks may be learned.

This project provides you with the information required to make two styles of yo-yo. The first uses a hole saw, the second utilizes ready-made wood wheels. The construction of both styles is quick and straightforward.

**CUTTING LIST**

Small pieces of 6mm (¼in) birch plywood
Wood wheels
Cord

## Construction

### Hole saw yo-yos

Cut two discs of 6mm (¼in) plywood using a hole saw. We recommend that you use the hole saw in conjunction with either a bench drill or a portable power drill attached to a drill stand. Your workpiece should be securely clamped when drilling.

If possible, select a slow to medium drill speed and feed the hole saw through the workpiece at a steady rate. It is advisable to have a clean scrap piece of wood underneath the workpiece to ensure that the hole saw does not cut into the drill table.

The size of the yo-yo will, of course, be dependent upon the diameter size of the hole saw blade that you use. We made ours 63mm (2½in) in diameter.

If necessary, drill out the centre hole of each disc with a 6mm (¼in) drill bit.

Prepare a length of 6mm (¼in) dowel. This will serve as the axle.

The length of the axle will depend upon the size of string you decide to use. We suggest a maximum width of 22mm (⅞in), and you will therefore require a 22mm (⅞in) length of 6mm (¼in) dowel. Our yo-yos were all this width.

Glue a disc to each end of the dowel axle.

The yo-yo may now be painted and decorated, and the string attached.

### Wheel yo-yos

The other type of yo-yo is made using ready-made wood wheels. These are available in various sizes, usually 25mm (1in) – 76mm (3in) in diameter.

Apart from light sanding, all you will need to do to these wheels is to drill out the axle holes to 6mm (¼in) diameter.

The chosen width of the yo-yo will again determine the length of 6mm (¼in) dowel you will need for the axle. We made a 38mm (1½in) diameter yo-yo 25mm (1in) wide; a 50mm (2in) diameter yo-yo 32mm (1¼in) wide; and a 63mm (2½in) diameter yo-yo 38mm (1½in) wide.

Assemble these yo-yos in the same manner as the hole saw ones. Finish and string them.

## Finishing

We painted the hole saw yo-yos and decorated them with dry rub-down shapes. The wheel yo-yos were stained using thinned acrylic paint.

## Stringing

The length of cord you use is entirely up to you. Choose a type that will allow the yo-yo to run smoothly.

When attaching the string, loop the cord around the axle and tie a knot. Then wind the cord around the axle a few times and tie another knot securely. With scissors or a knife, trim the surplus cord away. This process of attaching the cord will help prevent the yo-yo from slipping, thus not rewinding, during use.

Make and tie a finger loop at the other end of the cord.

Your yo-yo is now ready for play.

## Alternatives

The performance of the yo-yos can be altered by changing the axle diameters. Instead of using 6mm (¼in) dowel, experiment with larger diameters such as 10mm (⅜in) or 12mm (½in).

The yo-yos are an ideal project in which to involve children. They could have great fun experimenting with design, dimensions and manufacture.

# TWENTY-TWO

# Theatre

You can produce your own plays in miniature using this theatre. Recreate classical productions or use your imagination and write your own!

Like many other projects in this book, the theatre has been designed with storage and space considerations in mind. It can easily be dismantled and flat-packed away after use.

The characters are physically two-dimensional. They are each attached via a tenon to a base that allows a rod and handle to be fitted. By controlling the rod, the characters may be moved around the stage.

Undoubtedly you will want to design and make characters of your own choice, but to help get you started we have designed four characters: a prince, princess, wizard and ogre.

The removable backdrop of the theatre has scenery painted on it. Extra backdrops could be made displaying different scenes. A door (or doors) could be cut out of a backdrop, thereby adding an extra entrance/exit – vital if you intend to stage a farce!

You will notice that the size and scale of the theatre is relatively small. It can easily be enlarged if you require a bigger stage.

## CUTTING LIST

**Theatre**

| | |
|---|---|
| Curtains (2): | 300 x 152 x 12mm (11$^{13}$/$_{16}$ x 6 x $^1$/$_2$in) birch plywood |
| Backdrop: | 300 x 152 x 12mm (11$^{13}$/$_{16}$ x 6 x $^1$/$_2$in) birch plywood |
| Bracing beam (2): | 160 x 16 x 6mm (6$^5$/$_{16}$ x $^5$/$_8$ x $^1$/$_4$in) birch plywood |
| Stage: | 300 x 150 x 18mm (11$^{13}$/$_{16}$ x 5$^{29}$/$_{32}$ x $^3$/$_4$in) MDF or birch plywood |
| Shield: | 32 x 28 x 3mm (1$^1$/$_4$ x 1$^1$/$_8$ x $^1$/$_8$in) birch plywood |

**Characters**

Figures: various scraps of 3mm ($^1$/$_8$in) birch plywood

Character bases (all 10mm ($^3$/$_8$in) birch plywood):

| | |
|---|---|
| Prince: | 35 x 24mm 1$^3$/$_8$ x $^{15}$/$_{16}$in) |
| Princess: | 39 x 24mm (1$^9$/$_{16}$ x $^{15}$/$_{16}$in) |
| Wizard: | 60 x 24mm (2$^3$/$_8$ x $^{15}$/$_{16}$in) |
| Ogre: | 70 x 24mm (2$^3$/$_4$ x $^{15}$/$_{16}$in) |

**Handles**

(4) 254 x 5mm (10 x $^3$/$_{16}$in) diameter ramin dowel

(4) 18mm ($^3$/$_4$in) diameter wooden balls (preferably the type that have partly drilled 5mm ($^3$/$_{16}$in) holes)

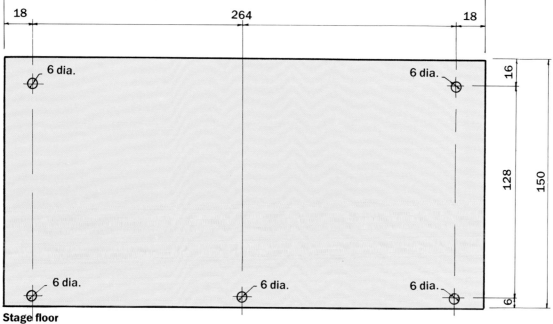

**Stage floor**
The five peg holes are drilled to a depth of 10mm ($^3$/$_8$in)

*Fig 22.1*
**Various components of the theatre.**

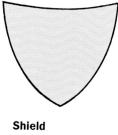

**Shield**
(Scale: full size)

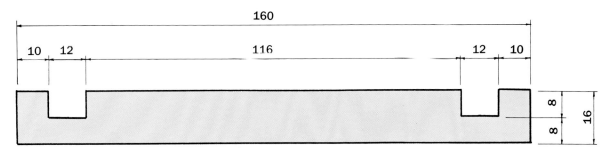

**Stage bracing beam (2)**

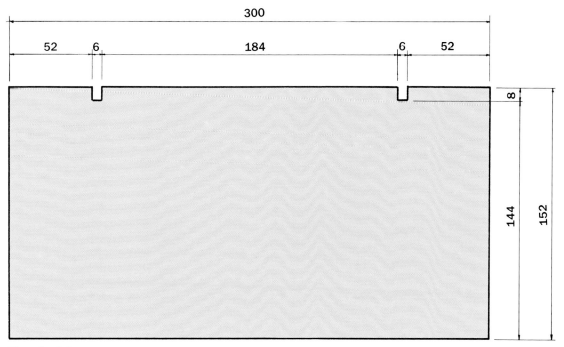

**Stage backdrop**

300

52          6                              184

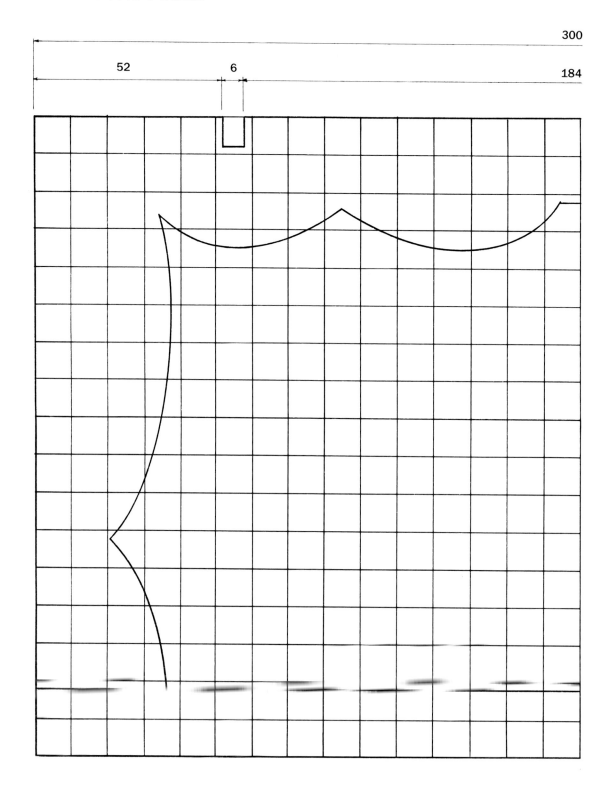

Fig 22.2

**Front elevation of base and curtains only.**

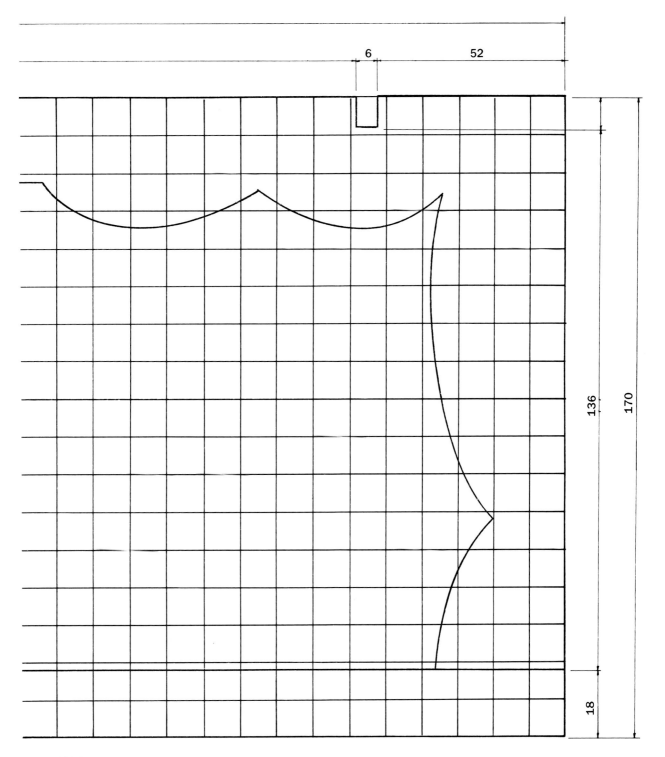

10mm (³⁄₈in) squares

6    52    136    170    18

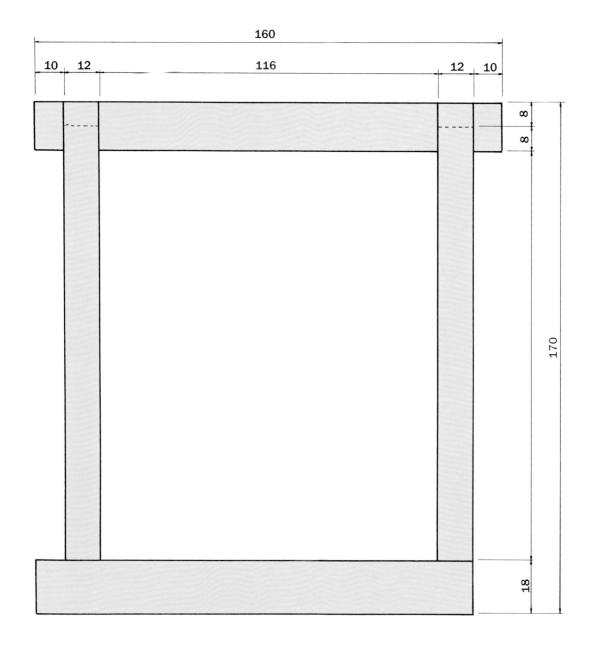

160

10 12 116 12 10

8

8

170

18

Fig 22.3
Side elevation of the assembled stage.

## Construction

### Theatre

Cut out and prepare all the components
(see **Figs 22.1–22.3**).

Glue the shield into place at the top of the
curtains.

Drill a central 6mm (¼in) diameter hole, 12mm
(½in) deep in the bottom of each of the side
curtains. Likewise, drill three of the same size
holes into the bottom edge of the backdrop
(one in the centre, the others 18mm (¾in) in
from each edge.

The stage bracing beams hold together the
front curtains and the backdrop by means of

Scale: full size

**Princess**

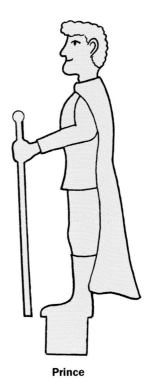

**Prince**

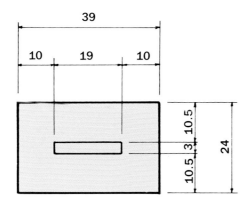

- All bases are 10mm (³⁄₈in) thick
- Each slot is cut all the way through
- For clarity, the handle rod hole details are not shown (see text for details)

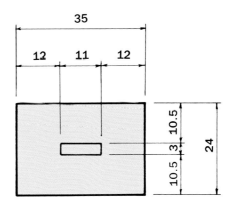

*Fig 22.4*
**The princess and prince and their bases.**

straightforward halving joints (see **Fig 22.1**). If heavy decoration (layers of paint, paper etc.) of these components is planned, allow for this when cutting the joints. This will ensure that the halving joints will not be too tight a fit.

Assemble the curtains, backdrop and beams. Place a centre point (see 'Dowel Joints' in the Construction Techniques chapter, page 17)

into each of the five previously drilled bottom holes. Now place this assembly onto the top surface of the stage piece. When it is correctly in position, press the assembly firmly down on the stage. This is so that the centre points make an impression.

Drill five 6mm (¼in) diameter holes, 12mm (½in) deep, into the top surface of the stage,

- Base is 10mm (³⁄₈in) thick
- See text for details of handle rod holes

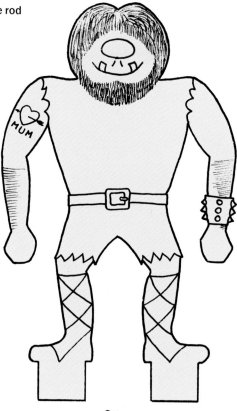

**Ogre**

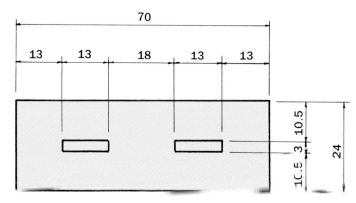

Fig 22.5
**The ogre and his base.**

using the impressions made by the centre points as the hole centres.

Take out the centre points from the theatre assembly. In their place, glue in five 25mm (1in) long ramin dowels.

Paint and decorate the theatre components as desired.

**Characters**

Transfer the characters onto 3mm (¹⁄₈in) plywood and cut them out (see **Figs 22.4 and 22.5**).

Cut out a base for each character.

Sand smooth any rough surfaces and edges.

Scale: full size

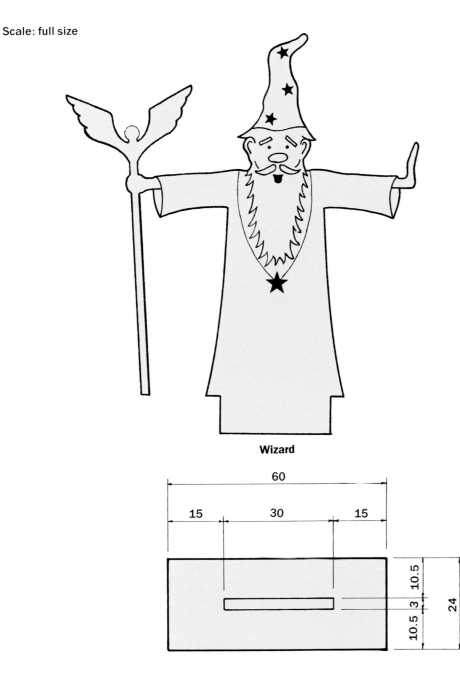

**Wizard**

60

15    30    15

10.5
3
10.5
24

*Fig 22.6*
**The wizard and his base.**

Glue the tenons of each character into their respective bases. Smooth away, with a block plane and abrasive paper, any protrusion that the tenons cause on the bottom face of the base.

Hold each character firmly in a vice and drill a 5mm (³⁄₁₆in) diameter hole centrally in each of the side faces of the base ends. These should

be drilled to a depth of 10mm (³⁄₈in).

Paint the characters.

Glue a wooden ball to one end of each controlling rod.

# TWENTY-THREE

# 18-Wheeler Lorry and Tractors

Most children like lorries, and should enjoy playing with this toy. In fact, during play testing this proved to be one of the most popular toys of the range described in the book! It was bashed, crashed and generally played with by many children!

Providing tractors for the lorry to haul has added extra play dimensions. It is possible to extend the play value even further in a number of ways. For example, the easy-to-attach Velcro securing straps allow the lorry to haul a variety of items (e.g. blocks, logs etc.). Also, a hook could be fixed onto the back of each tractor and attachments, such as grass cutters, harrowers, rollers etc., could be designed and made.

The scale of the project has been carefully thought out, utilizing ready-made 50mm (2in) diameter plastic wheels.

## CUTTING LIST

**Truck Cab**

| | |
|---|---|
| Chassis: | 248 x 98 x 18mm (9³/₄ x 3⁷/₈ x ³/₄in) plywood |
| Top interior block: | 98 x 25 x 18mm (3⁷/₈ x 1 x ³/₄in) plywood |
| Base interior block: | 98 x 74 x 30mm (3⁷/₈ x 2¹⁵/₁₆ x 1³/₁₆in) beech |
| Front panel: | 98 x 46 x 10mm (3⁷/₈ x 1²⁷/₃₂ x ³/₈in) plywood |
| Back panel: | 98 x 85 x 6mm (3⁷/₈ x 3³/₈ x ¹/₄in) plywood |
| Side panel (2): | 115 x 90 x 6mm (4⁹/₁₆ x 3⁹/₁₆ x ¹/₄in) plywood |
| Mudguard (2): | 90 x 48 x 3mm (3⁹/₁₆ x 1²⁹/₃₂ x ¹/₈in) plywood |
| Roof: | 77 x 98 x 10mm (3¹/₁₆ x 3⁷/₈ x ³/₈in) plywood |
| Front bumper: | 116 x 18 x 6mm (4¹⁹/₃₂ x ³/₄ x ¹/₄in) plywood |
| Rear bumper: | 120 x 20 x 6mm (4³/₄ x 1³/₁₆ x ¹/₄in) plywood |
| Diesel tanks (2): | 36 x 25mm (1⁷/₁₆ x 1in) dowel |

**Trailer**

| | |
|---|---|
| Flat bed: | 400 x 120 x 12mm (15³/₄ x 4³/₄ x ¹/₂in) plywood |
| Axle rod retainer block: | 125 x 72 x 39mm (4¹⁵/₁₆ x 2⁷/₈ x 1¹⁷/₃₂in) beech |
| Stand retainer: | 60 x 15 x 12mm (2³/₈ x ⁵/₈ x ¹/₂in) plywood |
| Hitching peg block: | 30 x 30 x 21mm (1³/₁₆ x 1³/₁₆ x ²⁷/₃₂in) beech |
| Tailgate: | 120 x 51 x 6mm (4³/₄ x 2¹/₃₂ x ¹/₄in) plywood |
| Stand leg (2): | 52 x 10 x 6mm (2⁷/₈ x ³/₈ x ¹/₄in) plywood |
| Leg brace: | 72 x 3mm (2⁷/₈ x ¹/₈in) diameter dowel |

**Tractor**

| | |
|---|---|
| Main body: | 130 x 44 x 30mm (5¹/₈ x 1³/₄ x 1³/₁₆in) beech |
| Side panel (2): | 84 x 60 x 12mm (3⁵/₁₆ x 2³/₈ x ¹/₂in) plywood |
| Roof: | 46 x 54 x 3mm (1²⁷/₃₂ x 2¹/₈ x ¹/₈in) plywood |

## MISCELLANEOUS MATERIALS

**Lorry**
(18) 50mm (2in) plastic wheels
(18) 5mm (³/₁₆in) spring hubcaps
Length of 5mm (³/₁₆in) diameter axle rod
(18) washers (to fit axle rod)

**Tractors (for each one)**

| | |
|---|---|
| Back wheels: | (2) 50mm (2in) plastic wheels (2) 5mm (³/₁₆in) spring hubcaps Length of 5mm (³/₁₆in) diameter axle rod |

(2) washers to fit axle rod

| | |
|---|---|
| Front wheels: | (2) 42 x 10mm (1²¹/₃₂ x ³/₈in) plastic wheels Length of 2mm (³/₃₂in) axle rod (2) hubcaps to fit axle rod Washers to fit axle rod |

**Velcro:** (2) lengths of 18mm (³/₄in) one self-adhesive, one sew-on.

## Construction

### Truck cab

The correct name for the lorry cab is 'tractor unit' but to save confusion with the actual tractors which this lorry carries we have referred to it as the 'truck cab' throughout these construction notes.

The key component of the truck cab is the chassis – most of the other components are either built onto or around it.

In toys of similar design, the axle rods are retained by two strips of timber attached lengthways to the chassis's underside. This project veers from the norm in that the axle rods pass right through the main chassis block itself. The reason for this is the desire to produce a more compact and neat cab unit. If the drilling of the axle holes through the width of the chassis presents a problem, alternative methods of construction are provided (see **Fig 23.4**).

Begin construction by cutting out all the components of the unit, with the exception of the diesel tanks.

Axle holes
Drill out the three axle rod holes through the side of the chassis (see **Fig 23.1**). An extra long 5mm (³⁄₁₆in) drill bit will be required to do this. Before drilling, make absolutely sure that the centres of all three holes run on the same parallel plane to the ground. If they do not, the wheels, when attached, will be uneven and will not all make contact with the ground! Ensuring that the plywood used is flat and not warped will aid this. Also, mark the horizontal middle of the three holes using a marking gauge set to half the thickness of the chassis.

It is advisable to drill the holes using a pillar drill, with the chassis securely held squarely in either a vice or similar clamping system.

With the holes drilled, pass the axle rods through the axle holes and place the appropriate number of wheels in the correct position. Then place this assembly onto a flat surface. This will allow you to check that all the wheels make contact with this surface before the assembly has gone too far.

If you have difficulty in passing the axle rods through the chassis holes, you can enlarge these holes by clamping the chassis in a bench vice and enlarging them using a standard (and of a marginally larger diameter) drill bit and hand drill. Remember that you will need to drill from both sides of the chassis.

Trailer retainer hole
Drill the trailer retainer hole in the chassis to a depth of 7mm (⁵⁄₃₂in). The location is shown in Fig 23.1. The diameter of this hole will need to be slightly larger than the trailer's hitching peg, so as to allow an easy fit

Mudguards
Glue each mudguard piece onto the cab side before cutting out the wheel arches (see **Fig 23.2**). The arches may then be cut out of the mudguards and cab side in one operation.

Driver's cab section
Glue and pin the two interior cab blocks together. Then glue the front piece of the cab to the interior block (see **Fig 23.3**).

To aid gluing, the components may be held together by pins until the glue has set. Then remove the pins.

Glue this assembly in place at the front end of the chassis. Remember, part A from Fig 23.3 is the front panel; this should help you position the assembly correctly before gluing. When the glue has set, clean up the sides with a combination of block plane and/or abrasive paper so that the newly attached component is squarely flush with the chassis sides.

Next, glue and pin the sides of the cab into position.

The roof component may now be glued and pinned into place.

Fix the back piece of the cab into place.

Drill the 'headlamp' holes into the front bumper with a 10mm (³⁄₈in) wood bit before gluing and pinning it into position (see **Fig 23.2**).

To produce a less angularly shaped cab, round some of the cab edges, especially the top corners of the roof and the bumper ends.

Pin and glue the rear bumper to the chassis and round off some of its edges and corners.

Diesel tanks
To make the two diesel tanks, plane a flat edge to the dowel being used. These flats should

be about 12mm (½in) in width. Cut out two tanks, each 36mm (1⅞in) in length. Glue and pin these into position with the flat side butted to the chassis (see **Fig 23.2**).

## Chassis alternative

If the chassis construction method described proves problematical, two alternatives are possible.

**1** Simply screw the wheels into place using

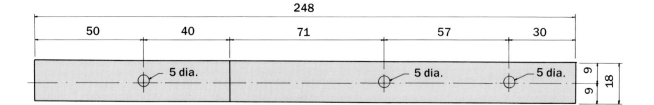

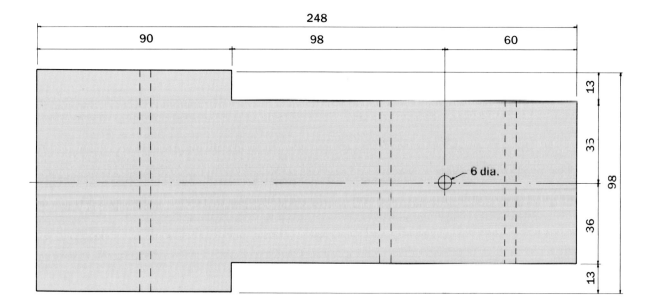

Fig 23.1
**Side and plan views of the chassis, the key
component of the truck cab.**

A Chassis
B Mudguard
C Side panel
D Roof
E Front bumper
F Rear bumper
G Diesel tanks
H Front panel

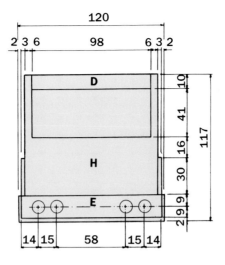

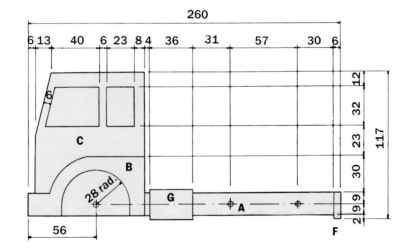

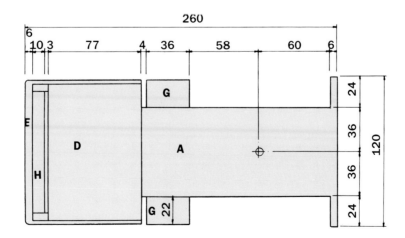

Fig 23.2
**Front, side and plan views of the truck cab
assembly.**

**159**

roundhead screws. The main drawback to this method is that the wheels are held less securely with screws than they are with axle rods.

**2** Make a chassis framework from separate plywood pieces. This will simplify the drilling of the axle holes. Fig 23.4 illustrates a suggested alternative chassis framework. The axle holes may then be drilled before the chassis is assembled. To ensure that these holes line up correctly, dry pin or tape the relevant opposing chassis side pieces together and drill through both in one operation.

## The trailer

The main component of the trailer is its 'flat bed', made from 12mm (½in) plywood (see **Fig 23.5**). After sanding it smooth, use a pencil and rule to divide the top surface with 10mm (⅜in) parallel lines running lengthways. Then go over them with a black Biro pen. These lines will later help create the illusion of planking.

Stain and varnish the top of the trailer. The choice of woodstain colour is entirely at your discretion, but do bear in mind that actual

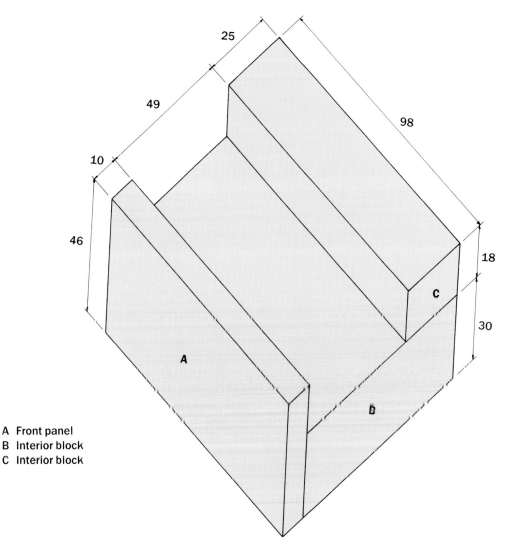

A Front panel
B Interior block
C Interior block

*Fig 23.3*
**The interior blocks and front panel form a unit that is attached to the truck cab chassis.**

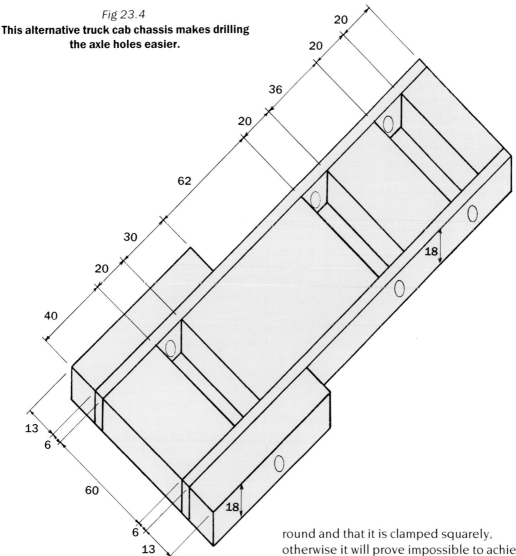

*Fig 23.4*
**This alternative truck cab chassis makes drilling the axle holes easier.**

truck/lorry trailer beds are usually of a dark shade. Also, ensure that the varnish you use will not react with the stain!

Cut out the large axle rod retainer block from a single block of beech or similar hardwood. Clean the sawn surfaces with a combination of plane (a shoulder plane is ideal) and abrasive paper.

Mark the centres of the axle rod holes in a similar manner as the cab's. Again, you will need to drill these holes with an extra long drill bit. The holes should be drilled using a pillar drill with the workpiece securely clamped to the drill's table. Make absolutely sure that the workpiece is square all the way

round and that it is clamped squarely, otherwise it will prove impossible to achieve accurate drilling. (For an alternative method, see page 15).

When finished, glue and cramp the axle retainer block to the underside of the trailer. If you wish, you could strengthen this join by dowel jointing the components together using 6mm (¼in) dowel pegs.

Fix a 34mm (1⅜in) length of 6mm (¼in) dowel through the centre of the hitching peg block, leaving a 7mm (⁹⁄₃₂in) length protruding from the underside and a 6mm (¼in) length protruding from the top.

Drill a 6mm (¼in) diameter hole to a depth of 6mm (¼in) into the underside of the trailer and glue the top peg of the hitching peg unit into this hole (see **Fig 23.5**).

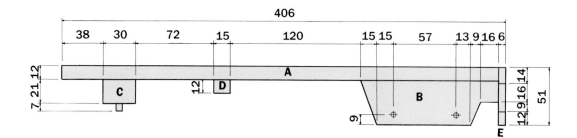

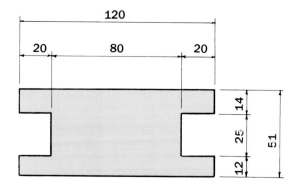

A Flat bed
B Axle stand retainer block
C Hitching peg block
D Stand retainer
E Tailgate

Fig 23.5
Side, rear and underside views of the trailer.

The collapsible trailer stand is made from two legs (see **Fig 23.7**), which are joined with a 72mm (2⅞in) length of 3mm (⅛in) dowel.

The top holes in each of the legs should be countersunk (on the outside face) to accept the head of a No. 4 x 18mm (¾in) brass screw.

The stand is retained to the underside of the

trailer by being screwed to a small securing block (see **Fig 23.5**). Before gluing and pinning this block *in situ*, it is advisable to put the screws' pilot holes into the ends. Also, ensure that you don't place the fixing pins too near the ends of the block, as this may hinder the fitting of the retaining screws.

Glue and pin the tailgate into position.

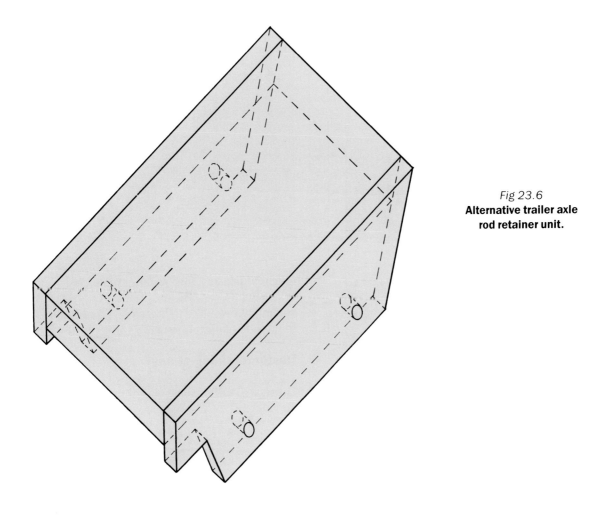

*Fig 23.6*
**Alternative trailer axle
rod retainer unit.**

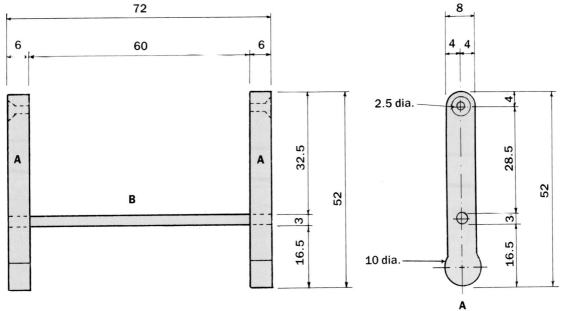

*Fig 23.7*
**The trailer stand consists of two stand legs** *(a)* **and
a leg brace** *(b)*.

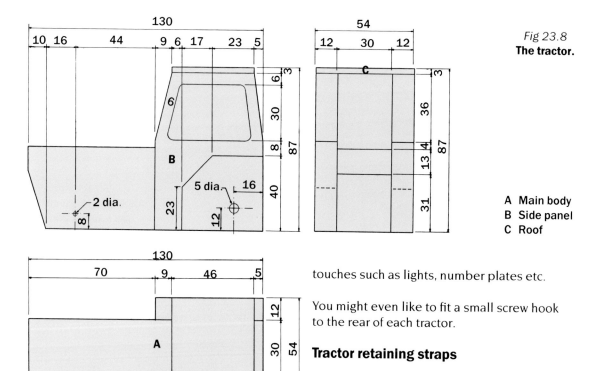

Fig 23.8
**The tractor.**

A  Main body
B  Side panel
C  Roof

## Axle rod retainer block alternative

If the construction and drilling of the block by the method given proves problematical, an alternative is illustrated in Fig 23.7. This is constructed of two side pieces, cut from 6mm (1/4in) plywood (dimensions the same as the side of the original block). Each is glued and pinned to a piece of 125 x 60 x 12mm (4¹⁵/₁₆ x 2³/₈ x ½in) plywood.

## Tractors

The tractors are relatively straightforward to make. Cut out all the components (see **Fig 23.8**). Drill the axle holes. Glue and pin the sides to the main bodies, then glue the tractor roofs into place.

If desired, slightly round the edges of the tractor bonnets to give a less angular effect.

## Finishing

Before fitting the wheels and the trailer stand, it is best to paint the project.

Use bright colours and add little finishing

touches such as lights, number plates etc.

You might even like to fit a small screw hook to the rear of each tractor.

## Tractor retaining straps

These are made using self-adhesive and sew-on Velcro.

Stick two lengths of the 'stick to' part of the self-adhesive Velcro to the underside of the trailer. Place one length as close to the outside edge as possible on one side, running from the position of the front end of the hitching peg block to the front end of the axle rod retainer block. Place the second length in the same position but on the other side of the trailer (see **Fig 23.9**). Also, place a 25mm (1in) length between each set of wheels.

For each tractor cut a 270mm (10⅝in) length of sew-on Velcro – only the 'soft' side is required. This is placed through the tractor cabs and sticks, at each end, to the Velcro placed on the underside of the trailer unit

Fig 23.9
**The 'stick to' part of the Velcro is adhered to the underside of the trailer.**

# Glossary

**axle** A spindle on which a wheel rotates, or which rotates with the wheel. Sometimes refers to a rod connecting two wheels.

**butt joint** (or **butted**) A simple joint where two parts to be joined are placed against each other, with no interlocking parts, and fixed.

**cam** A disc that is shaped to convert circular motion (in this book, the circular motion of wheels and axle arrangements) into variable or reciprocal motion.

**chamfer** (to chamfer) To produce a bevel on an edge.

**de-nibb** To lightly scour away, with a fine abrasive medium, any imperfections or general roughness from a finish, prior to applying the final coat.

**diameter** The length of a straight line passing through the centre of a circle, and touching the circumference of the circle at each end.

**dry assembly** A test assembly of components prior to final fixing with adhesive.

**end grain** After cutting across the fibres (or grain) of a piece of wood, the newly exposed surface is termed the end grain.

**follower** A component that has a surface that is either in constant or intermittant contact with the cam. It usually relays part, or all, of the cam's motion to a reciprocating component.

**jig** A device that enables a repetitive operation to be carried out, usually without the need for major adjustment and measurement.

**lug** A projecting piece (such as a peg or pin)

that is used for the location of one component to another.

**MDF** Medium-density fibreboard. Manufactured fibreboard with two smooth surfaces. In some instances, it may be used as a substitute for solid wood or plywood.

**mitre joint** Where two pieces of wood have each been cut at an angle, usually 45°, and joined.

**moulding** In the context of this book, a length of decorative edging usually made up from a series of curves and beads.

**off-centre** Not central. Symmetrically not balanced.

**offset** Similar to 'off-centre'. For example, if an axle of a wheel is not fitted centrally, it is offset.

**pare** The fine removal of wood shavings with a knife or chisel.

**PPI** Points per inch. Term used to denote how many saw tooth points there are per inch.

**rivet set** A metal tool that has a cuplike depression set into part of it that holds a rivet head while the other end of the rivet is worked with a hammer, or a combination of a hammer and another set.

**rivet shank** The cylindrical part of the rivet that is situated behind the rivet's convex head.

**washer** A flat metal disc, usually with a central hole, which is placed between components. In the case of this book, washers are used to alleviate friction between the bodies of toy vehicles and their wheels.

# Metric Conversion Table

| Inches to Millimetres and Centimetres | | | | | | |
|---|---|---|---|---|---|---|
| **MM** = Millimetres   **CM** = Centimetres | | | | | | |
| INCHES | MM | CM | INCHES | CM | INCHES | CM |
| ⅛ | 3 | 0.3 | 9 | 22.9 | 30 | 76.2 |
| ¼ | 6 | 0.6 | 10 | 25.4 | 31 | 78.7 |
| ⅜ | 10 | 1.0 | 11 | 27.9 | 32 | 81.3 |
| ½ | 13 | 1.3 | 12 | 30.5 | 33 | 83.8 |
| ⅝ | 16 | 1.6 | 13 | 33.0 | 34 | 86.4 |
| ¾ | 19 | 1.9 | 14 | 35.6 | 35 | 88.9 |
| ⅞ | 22 | 2.2 | 15 | 38.1 | 36 | 91.4 |
| 1 | 25 | 2.5 | 16 | 40.6 | 37 | 94.0 |
| 1¼ | 32 | 3.2 | 17 | 43.2 | 38 | 96.5 |
| 1½ | 38 | 3.8 | 18 | 45.7 | 39 | 99.1 |
| 1¾ | 44 | 4.4 | 19 | 48.3 | 40 | 101.6 |
| 2 | 51 | 5.1 | 20 | 50.8 | 41 | 104.1 |
| 2½ | 64 | 6.4 | 21 | 53.3 | 42 | 106.7 |
| 3 | 76 | 7.6 | 22 | 55.9 | 43 | 109.2 |
| 3½ | 89 | 8.9 | 23 | 58.4 | 44 | 111.8 |
| 4 | 102 | 10.2 | 24 | 61.0 | 45 | 114.3 |
| 4½ | 114 | 11.4 | 25 | 63.5 | 46 | 116.8 |
| 5 | 127 | 12.7 | 26 | 66.0 | 47 | 119.4 |
| 6 | 152 | 15.2 | 27 | 68.6 | 48 | 121.9 |
| 7 | 178 | 17.8 | 28 | 71.1 | 49 | 124.5 |
| 8 | 203 | 20.3 | 29 | 73.7 | 50 | 127.0 |

# About the Authors

Jeff Loader's woodworking career led him to help set up and run a wooden-toy-making workshop. This not only involved design and manufacture, but also the instruction of novices in various workshop practices and methods. Through this work he soon realized the love and joy of making, and playing with, wooden toys.

Jeff has written articles for various woodworking and modelling publications, as well as co-writing **Making Board, Peg and Dice Games** (GMC *Publications* Ltd) with his partner, Jennie.

Wooden toys and games apart, Jeff's many interests and activities include furniture design, restoring and using old woodworking tools, sport and playing (coping?!) with his young family.

Jennie Loader has a keen and active interest in many aspects of art, craft and design. She has studied photography and Leisure Management. To date her career has revolved around organizing drama, creative play, sporting and other pastime activities for varying groups of children, including those with special needs.

Jeff and Jennie were both born in the West Country and now live in Glastonbury with their two young children.

# TITLES AVAILABLE FROM GMC PUBLICATIONS LTD

## BOOKS

| | | | |
|---|---|---|---|
| Woodworking Plans and Projects | GMC Publications | Designing & Making Wooden Toys | Terry Kelly |
| 40 More Woodworking Plans and Projects | GMC Publications | Making Dolls' House Furniture | Patricia King |
| Woodworking Crafts Annual | GMC Publications | Making and Modifying Woodworking Tools | Jim Kingshott |
| Woodworkers' Career and Educational Source Book | GMC Publications | The Workshop | Jim Kingshott |
| Woodworkers' Courses & Source Book | GMC Publications | Sharpening: The Complete Guide | Jim Kingshott |
| Useful Woodturning Techniques | GMC Publications | Turning Wooden Toys | Terry Lawrence |
| Woodturning Projects | GMC Publications | Making Board, Peg and Dice Games | Jeff & Jennie Loader |
| Green Woodwork | Mike Abbott | The Complete Dolls' House Book | Jean Nisbett |
| Making Little Boxes from Wood | John Bennett | The Secrets of the Dolls' House Makers | Jean Nisbett |
| Furniture Restoration & Repair For Beginners | Kevin Jan Bonner | Wildfowl Carving: Volume I | Jim Pearce |
| Woodturning Jewellery | Hilary Bowen | Make Money from Woodturning | Ann & Bob Phillips |
| The Incredible Router | Jeremy Broun | Guide to Marketing | Jack Pigden |
| Electric Woodwork | Jeremy Broun | Woodcarving Tools, Materials & Equipment | Chris Pye |
| Woodcarving: A Complete Course | Ron Butterfield | Making Tudor Dolls' Houses | Derek Rowbottom |
| Making Fine Furniture: Projects | Tom Darby | Making Georgian Dolls' Houses | Derek Rowbottom |
| Restoring Rocking Horses | Clive Green & Anthony Dew | Making Period Dolls' House Furniture | Derek & Sheila Rowbottom |
| Heraldic Miniature Knights | Peter Greenhill | Woodturning: A Foundation Course | Keith Rowley |
| Practical Crafts: Seat Weaving | Ricky Holdstock | Turning Miniatures in Wood | John Sainsbury |
| Multi-centre Woodturning | Ray Hopper | Pleasure and Profit from Woodturning | Reg Sherwin |
| Complete Woodfinishing | Ian Hosker | Making Unusual Miniatures | Graham Spalding |
| Woodturning: A Source Book of Shapes | John Hunnex | Woodturning Wizardry | David Springett |
| Making Shaker Furniture | Barry Jackson | Adventures in Woodturning | David Springett |
| Upholstery: A Complete Course | David James | Furniture Projects | Rod Wales |
| Upholsterer's Pocket Reference Book | David James | Decorative Woodcarving | Jeremy Williams |
| Upholstery Techniques and Projects | David James | | |

## VIDEOS

| | | | |
|---|---|---|---|
| Ray Gonzalez | Carving a Figure: The Female Form | **Dennis White Teaches Woodturning** | |
| David James | The Traditional Upholstery Workshop Part I: Stuffover Upholstery | Part 1 | **Turning Between Centres** |
| David James | The Traditional Upholstery Workshop Part II: Drop-in and Pinstuffed Seats | Part 2 | **Turning Bowls** |
| | | Part 3 | **Boxes, Goblets and Screw Threads** |
| | | Part 4 | **Novelties and Projects** |
| John Jordan | Bowl Turning | Part 5 | **Classic Profiles** |
| John Jordan | Hollow Turning | Part 6 | **Twists and Advanced Turning** |
| Jim Kingshott | Sharpening the Professional Way | | |
| Jim Kingshott | Sharpening Turning and Carving Tools | | |

GMC Publications regularly produces new books and videos on a wide range of woodworking and craft subjects, and an increasing number of specialist magazines, all available on subscription:

## MAGAZINES

**WOODCARVING      WOODTURNING      BUSINESSMATTERS**

All these publications are available through bookshops and newsagents, or may be ordered by post from the publishers at 166 High Street, Lewes, East Sussex BN7 1XU, telephone (0273) 477374, fax (0273) 478606. Credit card orders are accepted.

**PLEASE WRITE OR PHONE FOR A FREE CATALOGUE.**